BEST *of* AUSTRALIAN POEMS 2021

First published 2021 by
Australian Poetry
www.australianpoetry.com

National Library of Australia
Cataloguing-in-Publication data:

Best of australian poems 2021
ISBN: 978-0-9923189-2-5

Printed by Lightning Source International
Design: Sophie Gaur

Publisher Note:
AP would like to deeply thank all the publishers, platforms, and other organisations that support
the flourishing and publishing of Australian poetry. While some of these *BoAP 2021* poems were
selected in open call-out, many were previously published by these great forces. It is AP's policy
as Publisher to also keep 'arm's length' completely in the selection of poems by our guest editors,
where we have different guest editors across our numerous, annual publications. In this, we respect
both their autonomy, but this also creates a trustful, ethical process. AP's house style is to accept
a poet's choice of punctuation, titling and spelling styles (outside converting hypens to dashes),
so across the book there is a 'natural' variation in poets' choices. Finally, a number of patrons
have contributed funds to this particular project, in its inaugural iteration. To these, and our core
funders and project partners, profound thanks.

This project has been assisted by the Australian Government through the Australia Council, its arts
funding and advisory body.

BEST *of* AUSTRALIAN POEMS 2021

GUEST EDITORS

ELLEN VAN NEERVEN

&

TOBY FITCH

Australian Poetry

Best of Australian Poems

SERIES PUBLISHER
Australian Poetry

Acknowledgement of Country

Australian Poetry is based in Naarm, Melbourne, working in offices and remotely on both Wurundjeri Woi Wurrung and Boon Wurrung lands. We acknowledge their Elders, past, present, and emerging. As a national poetry body, we also acknowledge that we work across many lands, and communities, and we extend our deep respect to all First Peoples, not just in Australia, but across the globe, including poets and audiences, and their enduring connection to Country. We also acknowledge US poet laureate Joy Harjo's tribal nation, the Mvskoke Nation.

Foreword

[...] everybody will think the same at the same time... let us repeat now... I love my country... it starts with poetry... the big publisher abandons me... the business model abandons difference, poetry, marginality... we want sales... the literature as a business, a commodity... the airport book... the page turner... don't be too difficult now... speak to everybody... the lowest common denominator... we want simple form, we want a series, tv show and a film and sale of toys and trinkets... the whole shebang, says the accountant... because we lost the book subsidy... because we lost the policy... because we lost culture... the palace of culture now... the syndicated press, the bland voice that says reality television talk... the blah blah blah [...]

—Ania Walwicz, *from* 'WHAT HAPPENED TO BOOKS?'

The act of writing is an aural event.

—Ania Walwicz

In late September 2020, one of Australia's great performance poets and teachers of poetry Ania Walwicz died. Born in Poland in 1951, and emigrating to unceded Wurundjeri Woi Wurrung and Boon Wurrung lands in 1963, her distinctive voice and work embodied a migrant perspective of her adopted Australia ('the big ugly') through experimental prose and uncanny performances. She was a sound poet who took many of her cues from experimental music, such as that of John Cage, and, while her influence will be felt into the future, the loss of her anarchic feminist Dada alter egos now leaves a considerable gap in the Australian poetry community. And yet, with this in mind, we hope that Walwicz's spirit of persistence, critical eye, aesthetic experimentation and strident vocalisation from the margins can be felt in many of the 'aural events' of this poetry anthology.

Best of Australian Poems 2021 is the first anthology of what Australian Poetry, the national poetry organisation, hopes will be a longstanding series. Since Black Inc.'s highly regarded *Best Australian Poems* series concluded after its

2017 iteration, AP found there was considerable interest among both poets and readers in the idea of a new annual series. What *Best of Australian Poems (BoAP)* aims to do is collect together some of the 'best', most interesting, most challenging work by Australian poets of a twelve months' timeframe (in this case, July 2020–June 2021), and by doing so chart the waves and currents of each passing year. Another aim is that these anthologies will provide a space where new authors are discovered. With two different editors each year, this allows the series to broaden its scope and read as widely as possible. It also means that, with rotating editors, the series can evolve with each year, examining more ways to represent the fluctuating nature and poetics of what is being written throughout Australia's intertwining poetry communities.

In this volume you will find formal poems, prose poems, lyric and anti-lyric poems; list poems, documentary and archival poems, and poems derived from journal writing; spoken word or slam poetry, sound poetry, and other poems sourced from performance; protest poems, ecopoetry; translations and poems making use of other languages, including First Nations languages; digital poetry, visual poems, ekphrastic poetry, surrealist, collage and conceptual poetry; long poems, short poems, prize-winning poems; love poems, narrative poems, elegies and epistolary poems; ars poetica, collaborative poems, and more.

These various modes and forms cover a huge array of subjects, too. Here we have poems about family, mortality, and travel; poems about science, historical events and history repeating itself; poems critiquing or challenging colonialism, racism, the patriarchy, capitalism, and other systems of power; poems contending with religion, spirituality and mythology; poems about the body; expressions of gender; explorations of the abject; poems that repurpose public language and discourse; poems that look inward (about a locale, a memory, or a feeling) and poems that look outward (to the geopolitical, or the Anthropocene); poems about plants and animals and our relationships with them; and, of course, poems about fire and poems about the pandemic. And while we were drawn to topical poems, as this is an anthology of a very specific time period, the ones that stood out managed to balance timeliness with timelessness; their subjectivity with an attention to form and technique; or they alluded deftly to the matter at hand rather than spell it out—although there was certainly a place for poems that do not mince words.

With a huge inbox of many thousands of poems, we had more than enough to choose from—over half of the poems in this anthology come from poets who formally submitted—but we didn't rest there. We read dozens of individual poetry collections, from chapbooks to full-length and selected collections, and we have poets in the anthology representing most Australian publishers of poetry. We read as many Australian journals, magazines and newspapers that contain poetry—whether handmade publications, in print or online; small, medium or large—as we could, and international publications. And we perused exhibitions that included poetry, listened to poetry podcasts and seminars, and watched poetry performances. And while a majority of poems here have been previously published in the last year, we also have a significant portion of unpublished poems written in that timeframe. It would be disingenuous for us to say that we read every single poem written by Australian poets in the last year. Such a task is almost impossible. And there are barriers that prevent certain work being read—poems that exist in continuing oral traditions, poems from the streets, rallies, theatres, in the home, communities. There's value in work outside (this) establishment and we acknowledge that we are inevitably limited by our definitions of poetry.

In reading as editors for this anthology, conducting numerous meetings over Zoom, we attempted to broaden our own definitions of poetry, and in doing so we struck a symbiotic relationship with each other. We brought differing and overlapping reading expertise to the project, and we were able to remain open to each other's varying poetic preferences, something we believe is important to such a process and which was vital in finalising our editorial decisions.

And so, the poems we have settled on come from poets of a broad range of backgrounds, ages, genders, and from all states and territories and some expats overseas, providing a wide-reaching cross-section of Australian poetry that includes many of Australia's most accomplished and longstanding poets.

One other thing we can say about this cross-section is that it shows how a groundswell of younger generations are turning to poetry and producing work of high quality. Perhaps we could put that down to a combination of the prominence of creative writing programs across the country, whether at tertiary institutions or in communities; of an explosion of independent online magazines often run by editors and writers who have created their own writing communities, providing space and opportunity for those overlooked by larger publications; of a growing awareness that contemporary poetry can give a voice to the marginalised. Perhaps it reflects a world seeming ever more finite due to climate change, the pandemic and increasing geopolitical unrest; how writers might be turning to poetry—its ability to crystallise emotion, experience, truth and political valency—so as to subvert the dominant channels of public discourse such as television, social media, and the news media, all run as they are by global conglomerates with little interest (beyond their own profit and power) in a sustainable future for all. The urgency of the poetry in this anthology has things to say about all of this.

To find a structure for these 100 poems, admittedly a miscellany, we thought through a range of ordering principles and settled on presenting the poems in alphabetical order by title. This will give many of the poets a different sense of how their work can sit in an anthology (some poets' surnames finding them always appearing up front or at the end of anthologies). But mostly, we found that in this particular sequencing there were just more interesting resonances between poems, and that the more significant poems are neatly spaced out across the book. There is a fortuitous bookending to the collection, too, with visual poems at either extremity, which we hope will draw readers in at the beginning and send them away thinking about the possibilities and complexities of poetic form at the end.

We would like to thank every poet who submitted and who worked hard to publish across 2020–21. Australian poetry is in great health at present and it is impossible with anthologies such as this to include every excellent poem or poet. There were of course poets who could not be represented, either because they did not publish in the timeframe, did not submit new work or withdrew their work from consideration. We would like to thank AP, in particular Jacinta Le Plastrier, Emma Caskey and designer Sophie Gaur (working across massive time differences) for all their work assisting in the making of this book. It has been a privilege to read and consume (intensely) so much intense and wonderful poetry, and we hope you as readers will find poems in here that inspire, provoke and challenge your understanding of the world, and of poetry itself.

In the intervening period since the end of Black Inc.'s *Best Australian Poems*, a few significant Australian poets have passed away. We would like to honour the lives and poetic careers of those we can, at the moment of writing this:

Candy Royalle (1981–2018), Les Murray (1938–2019), Clive James (1939 –2019), Aunty Kerry Reed-Gilbert (1956–2019), Ania Walwicz (1951– 2020), Bruce Dawe (1930–2020) and Kate Jennings (1948–2021), and encourage readers to seek out their poems.

Finally, we would like to acknowledge the traditional custodians of the lands on which this work was edited and produced, the Awabakal, Yagera, Turrbal, Gadigal, Wiradjuri, Boon Wurrung and Wurundjeri Woi Wurrung First Nations peoples. These lands were never ceded. Always was, always will be Aboriginal land.

—*Toby Fitch and Ellen van Neerven*

POEMS

uncertainty   is   a   virus

        we must   all   be prepared
art   is   a virus
                                        love   is   a virus
        the economy   is   a virus
                                America   is a   virus
panic is   a   virus   essential   services are   a virus   anyone who still has a job
        is   a virus   we're all in this together   is a virus   all Australians
are   a   virus   the PM's tie is   awaiting results
        kindness   is   a   virus   the vulnerable   are   a virus
        condemnation   is   widespread   emotion is a virus   your friends are a   virus
help is   a virus   the virus is running out of gloves   cities are   a   virus
global warming   is   a   virus acceleration is a virus   the virus is   adapting the virus
is learning to tweet   Mel Gibson   is   a virus   bitcoin is a virus   Trump is a   pandemic
resilience   is a virus   empty shelves   are a   virus   singing is a virus   flash mobs are a virus
hugging   is a virus wear   a chicken mask instead   racism is a virus   old age   is a virus youth   is a
virus invincibility is a virus the virus is obsessed with Bill Gates   the virus is   working around
the clock   the virus   is upskilling   parliament   is   a virus   tik-tok is a virus back to business
is a virus   normal   is a virus   the virus is missing   its grandparents the virus has lost track of
days memory is a virus 20 seconds is a   virus   it is impossible to   catch a virus   if you always
wear a beard   cruise ships are a virus dancing is a virus healing is a   virus stupid is a virus   the
public are a virus the people are a   virus the virus is making the most of it the virus has never been so
clean compassion is a virus the health system   is a virus my beloved sharks are a virus   I'm
just waiting for the virus   to take this seriously eugenics are a virus individuals were otherwise
healthy the virus has unfriended me the virus is drawing the line   data is a virus conspiracy is a
virus resistance is a virus   please do not comment as this virus is no longer live stress is a virus
challenge is a virus explanations are against the rules changing your clothes is against the virus
changing your mind is against the rules hesitation is a virus spitting is a virus recovery is a virus
the virus can't believe what is happening of all the ways the world sings to me this one stuffs its fists
in my mouth the virus   is drowning the virus is looking to the future respiration is a virus mutation is
a virus behaviour is a virus time is a virus the virus is inside us   the virus knows nothing has changed

A Muslim, Christmas | OMAR SAKR

The streets are empty-ish.
Ish is for my body
the faithless and lonely.
I head toward departure.
Long one-eyed spectres
hunch over the earth
and each tree has around it
a darker deeper life.
Few shops are open: solitary
yellows adorn a doorway or two
amid dormant heavens
(I call any abundance heaven now) saying
welcome in Mandarin and later, Arabic.
I move past the beckoning oasis.
I am not looking for a home
all prior attempts failed—
I aim to find the heaven of me,
the we who linger at stations
to hear a loop of human voices
skip over silence or sink into it,
to relish the ripple that makes absence
visible. We move through enormity
and feel our crowdless edges
with the hand of an ancestor, perhaps
brushing the backs of our necks so
we tilt up to see a migrantory heaven
pummel the sky and disappear.
Elsewhere, beloveds
gather, ready to unwrap
a gift beneath
the semblance of a tree
or the memory of pine, still green,
and though I have one
a family I mean a queerness
I cannot abide leaving
the city without a body
to trouble its making.

I have no destination
in mind—how sacred it is,
this not knowing, how divine
to walk in this world as an ish.

Actually Existing Australia | LOUIS KLEE

Pale ankles in the mountains, divergences
on a quarry. We are witness to it
land and witness to it
some fact of further summer
or things a truck driver might say
                         'Ossa ashiver
              and no one knows why
speaking, coughing: it is a throat, after all, writing
poems is nothing like gladness.
Take posture, gesture from the rib
how the body is—it is hard
here shrubs heave like lungs, the young
men fly in, flown in quarry throat-deep folly
so it happens. Black glass
of the vitrified brain, in the earth-shaft
critique in pure resin, boiled stone; no time
is ever resolved and still we find it
in ore, grate it as glass, itemise it as
sand, grind it until it's suave as paste.
A poem hardly written.

Note: The phrase 'no time is ever resolved' comes from a speech by Jeanine Leane delivered in January 2020 at the University of Cambridge. It is sometimes attributed by Alexis Wright to Carlos Fuentes.

you wanted me to make some recommendations to you as to
whose poetry in australia is interesting enough to be
translated into chinese?
i'm not sure whether you are more interested in the past or the present
take the present okay?
there are big names of course
but you don't start with them or else you get stuck with them
start with small
things that have never been published
that are never allowed into print
oh yes what do you think australia is?
paradise? there is censorship believe me
about as bad as china and anywhere else
the only difference is they have a different name for it
they call it standards or quality
but you know what I call it?
I call it mediocrity whose name is australian poetry
avoid at any cost publications by major publishers
who don't know a thing about how to handle poetry except as a
marketing product
and whose main concern is the name
you still want the names?
you don't need me to tell you
they are there in every recent anthology
they are in the oxford companion of aust. lit.
or the cambridge hist. of aust. lit.
those who take up more pages than others
ask yourself these questions
why the others are never there
the Other that is
and if there ever is an anthology of unpublished australian poetry
a history of australian literary exclusions
and absences
why the worst still sits on top
and shits on others the Other that is
you still need the names?
i'm not a name dropper although i think i know a lot of them

save it for posterity
recommendations i don't have
not ever
and perhaps the only one i ever have is this:
find whatever that appeals to you at first sight
like love
and discard the rest
which is too much these days
bear in mind though
that poetry doesn't make money
even in a multimodern postcultural colonialpost
2nd class country
or go to a poet or critic at melb. uni.

Albedo | *LUKE BEESLEY*

The aeroplane twitched away from my window.
Its underbelly a sea anemone or exhumed pippy.

We were close enough to see the pilot, who did a filmic
wave—old cinema, the image jumping and cartoonish,

too fast. In fact, I was asked to slow down. I could see a whole
bird between the lines, but it was a piece of metal anyway.

It dropped away. No peg could hold it. Two of the lines were new.
They appeared fully formed, sloping to meet the one below

my eye that I had had since my early twenties. I put it down
to the lobster I watched in the early hours of Sunday morn.

The engine was cooked. What else? The first groans
of the garbage truck, which worked better than any alarm.

I kept turning over a lizard in my sleep to admire its white
chocolate. Much the same. It too twitched and disappeared.

ANNEAL | heat-up and cool down slowly; soften and strengthen to eliminate stress that accumulates through time; forge an open response to resist and shape-shift without losing one's essence.

---

mine and refine this float of molten landscape   raw silica-sand and limestone sites   sliced and stirred and hot-shop forged   we witness excavations of targets and melts   a redaction of origins of lives   of lands
                    see what a breath can do

flux and bubble   rise to fever-point and sweat   hot flesh on flesh   so carefully laid   rested and hung   body-broken to sway   see their shadows cast low in the sun   just *what they wanted*   what a breath   what breath
                    see what her sorrow can do

what a love   a brave pure love   this one grain of sand that refuses to disappear   the slightest fissure to rupture and dissect an unbearable fantasy facade   she seeks heartbeats and bloodlines   she exhumes humanity   assembles beauty to nurture and grow
                    see what her love can do

our screams soar into mighty blue
skies   dust to dust   bury them
deep   we scratch up to the
surface   all flesh cinder and
ash   their charred revelation   what
we've always known   their silence
translucent   she is patient   she
waits   she inhales and
exhales   she waits
                see what her breath can do

recognise this breath   gifted
from Old Ones   lessons afloat
in the wake of time   a warm
breeze-like   dance   on   shards   of
shadow and light   navigate
their caress   the gentlest
of touch   she will hold their breath-
deep   for as long as it takes   for
as long as it takes   to furnace and
shape you a story
                see what a breeze can do

a perfect wall of brittle display   a
cultivation of whiteness   stolen
and displaced   she seeks paper
and blood   where bodies are
traced she gathers them near   this
suitcase of breaths   to one day
rest   she carries in case   in her
case   in her
                let us see what they can do

these shimmering dreams   not
what they seem   a fallout mirage
of epic distortion   from
furnace to fission and shrouds of
black mist   to poisonous
shards of green-to-black   we
bear witness   to defiant life   to
a mass of destruction   to her
fruits her life   to her body her
strength her blood

      now see what her breath can do

The man next to me on the train has a swastika tattooed on his left forearm; three empty seats to my left.
The man next to me on the train is wearing a green and yellow t-shirt of the Australian cricket team.
The man next to me on the train catches me looking, checking, making sure my history isn't deceiving me.
I avert my gaze. History tucked into a back pocket.

> (English-speaking, jeans-made-in-China, op-shop green converse shoes, never-seen-a-shtetl-or-a-pogrom, lives-with-a-housemate-on-a-diet-of-toast-and-bananas: third culture Jew)

The man next to me on the train has other stuff tattooed on his left forearm but they don't bear repeating so I won't.

> (A fascist on the fremantle line)

I hear Grandma whisper something in my ear about how symbols chase
> & pounce

Questions for grandma:
Do they chase us or do we chase them?
Who do they pounce on?
How hard?
In this interspecies metaphoric paradigm, are fascists clawed or pawed creatures?

The day after the election, Dad and I run a half-marathon together
We cross the finish line hands lifted to the sky in celebration
I am wearing my 350 t-shirt
By '350', I mean 350 parts per million, that is, the amount scientists have agreed is the safe limit of carbon dioxide in our atmosphere.

> (when i was 16 i was obsessed with this number).

Every time we pass a group of random people on the side of the roads watching the race go past, we go full performance spectacle.
Dad and I whoop and cheer and wave, like we are champions.
I hold my shirt out.

> somewhere around the 8 kilometre mark dad murmurs: 'yes, 350, that'll be a museum piece. long gone now, 400, 410?...'

The morning of the 2019 election,
handing out how-to-vote cards at morley primary school,
on the way riding my bike through wide suburban tree-lined streets & white picket fences,
feeling like Democracy Oprah,
every house I pass yelling:
      '**you** get to vote! and **you** get to vote! and **you** get to vote!'
democracy sausage smell wafting through the air,
through the facade of choice,
as we all line up to play the game.

That night,
watching the country becoming blue,
magicians turn over cards,
and we are dazed, like we didn't even see him put one card behind his back,
shuffle the deck, rigged like so, pick out more from his top hat...

But i digress / detour / delineate / deliberate / devastate.

The playwright at the panel on theatre and politics says artists shouldn't talk about their feelings in public political spaces:
      "We don't want to hear it, stick to the facts", she says.
But I'm sad, I wanna yell. Aren't you?

Dad is an agricultural plant scientist,
He goes to a meeting in Seattle,
and talks to other scientists about food security.
'How was it?' I ask.
      'The other scientists were mostly wheat experts', he says.
      'Most wheat cycles last ten years. They joked that we're 3-6 wheat cycles
      'til the end of the world.'
 'Right',
My feet dangling off the side of the wooden bridge at Baigup Wetlands,
meaning 'place of rushes',
the Derbal Yerrigan river murmuring softly below.
A yellow-billed spoonbill digs digs digs.

Eduardo Kohn says all living beings think.
Animals, plants, forests, spirits
—all living beings forming habits, using signs to make sense of the world
around them, of their world—that this pattern forming is *what makes life a*
semiotic process".
> *"All life forms continuously engaged in appearing to one another in a process*
> *of sign making."*
That the tick differentiates between mammals and reptiles for survival,
That the ant eaters' snout is shaped like the burrows of the termites it feasts on,
That pumas don't eat you if you're lying sleeping face up,
because then it sees another self, another being.
sign-reading / sign-making / misconstrued signs / misreading

(i don't know what any of this means)
(contradictions? interspecies love?)
(they are just signs after all?)

as Fremantle fascist and I look at each other, across three empty train seats

[The quotes come from the book *"How Forests Think: Towards an Anthropology beyond the*
Human" by Eduardo Kohn (2013), published by University of California Press.]

Arrival | KRISTEN LANG

The dawn is flame-coloured. Where I have slept,
under trees, my indent still presses on the ground. I lean
into wakefulness, drawn above the mesh of the night:
the leaf falling, the child saying my name, the cobweb
stretched on my cheekbone. In the loose soil
my footprint stays without me, woven into the scent
of the morning. Wind trips through its coils of swell.
At my side, a black-backed beetle probes the leaf
that has fallen, shifting it with its hooked hands, a self-
styled flag. I gaze and so much blooms and spills
though it's I who emerges. Two wrens. So close
I can hold, with my lungs, their sheer hearts, their blue-
splashed heads. Where they flit, my fingers slide
into the yellow grass, and the white rims of the dew's
strung spheres cling to me, their clean, clear weight
lifting as I move, their suck dissolving into air
with that slow, slow levitation. Drifts of cloud
in the leaves of peeling gums, white on the white
trunks, feed on the dew's tide, lingering as it rises.
The child grows still, staring where her father's hand
gestures at a curving branch. Head-swivel of an owl. I lean.
Into the time I have. Wingbeats. Atoms of air. Soil
and tree-bark. A girl's pulse in the browns, the greens,
the yawning blues of a sky-dazzled land. The day rolls,
the world tumbles through me. In the wave of its momentum.

i.   I know myself to reach any destination ten to fifteen minutes faster than Google Maps will ever believe of me. My boyfriend calls it *gay pace*. I can't help it. I have places to be, and more places not to be. Everywhere, I'm early.

ii.   The late José Muñoz begins *Cruising Utopia* by telling us, *Queerness is not yet here.*

iii.   A quick search on Urban Dictionary describes gay pace as *the incredibly fast rate at which gay couples progress their relationships.* A slightly more drawn-out search suggests we walk gay pace for fear of judgement, or attack. A confidence coach said this. *Perceived risk*, is what she said.

iv.   Ten years ago I'd throw my body between knife fights in Northbridge. Those three a.m. heroics: they slow us down. Somehow, I always talked them out of it a hundred or so seconds before police would dare arrive. Why, at my most precarious, did I feel indestructible? Still—is it too much to ask for an innocence that makes men drop their weapons?

v.   I've either become wiser, or more fragile—
which I suppose aren't mutually exclusive
things, even if it feels like they ought to be.

vi.   Now, as I remind myself how to drive, I'm working hard to beat that *flight-flight* panic of approaching cars and faces as they reach me in the rear-view mirror. I have to constantly remind myself that this is just how traffic works. Everything is just movement across networks, through space. The inner map I make of unrecognised faces.

vii.   On the drive to Girrawheen Senior High, a woman on classical f.m. tells me that it only takes sixty seconds for a blood cell to circuit the whole body, and all I can think is: *How dare. The nerve.*

viii. Cells are constantly moving, HIV is constantly multiplying, antiretrovirals are constantly suppressing, borders are constantly extending. Every environment can safely be described as *hostile*.

ix. At the school, I try to teach the students about tempo, and I realise that I've begun to think of them as *mine*. To me, they seem so indestructible.

x. Donna Haraway keeps reminding me to *stay with the trouble*, except I'm wondering if the movement is the trouble.

xi.   (I very rarely read critical theory past the introduction.)

xii. Every time a man on Grindr walks into my home, it is with the awareness that I'm putting myself at risk of murder or of harm. The way we trade in false proximities. This is how they bind us: perhaps we truly put ourselves at risk of care.

xiii. Kinship: another *perceived risk*.

xiv. Someone told me recently that they had never really considered what borders meant, until they closed. I tell them that when I was diagnosed positive, I eventually came to realise there was nowhere I could go but home.

xv. At Galup, I force myself to slow to look at birds. *Arrival* has so many other meanings by the lake. Just three or so kilometres around. I am trying to find in circumnavigation some sense of Queer belonging, what Elizabeth Freeman describes as *persisting over time*. Inside me, everything I claim to know spreads a little further away. Where best to fall within that rippling diagram?   To be Queer is to understand you have been someplace you will never return. In a few months' time, I might wait to see the children hatch. The way ducklings learn to swim: zooming to their mothers in impossible bursts. Baby birds always feel as if they're mine, especially in the way they speed away.

This work draws on and refers to three texts: José Esteban Muñoz, *Cruising Utopia: the then and there of queer futurity* (New York University Press, 2009); Donna Jean Haraway, *Staying with the Trouble: making kin in the Cthulucene* (Duke University Press, 2016); and Elizabeth Freeman, *Time Binds: queer temporalities, queer histories* (Duke University Press, 2010).

a name: ancestor,
a thread i answer
at last—

sister says, what if
they think you are
full-blooded filipino?

spanish surnames
conjure colonies,
at least for us—

> (i have origamied
> a name out
> of shape before
>
> made my mouth
> a winded thing,
> for who?)

i am still learning
to parse a body
out of theory

let me let go of
the old white lie—
water in blood

> (after all, isn't
> australia also
> a name
>
> enacted,
> tacked on like
> an afterthought?)

remember: southern
land, white history
erases nothing—

there is still every
before / before
/ before

     (assimilation is
     not my mistaken
     mispronounced

     name is not any
     body's name is not
     whitewashed country)

so i begin with a name:
trace it, coil my tongue,
a river threading

back
back / back
back.

Aum Shinrikyo Farms Sarin | DAMEN O'BRIEN

The sneer of a desiccated sheep
peels back from its long jaw like
a gaunt connoisseur of grass.

The farmers of Banjawarn station
move through the dry fields
in spacesuits and gas masks

like the muzzles of mad rams
drunk on ragweed or thistle,
the farmers snort through their filters.

Far away Tokyo buzzes in
monochrome rushes of commuters
marking the future stations of their cross.

The sky expands under the flatline
of a Western Australian haze.
Boyle's Law for a gas holds here:

it's an empty laboratory, full of silence,
the vast ignorances of neighbours
fenced out kilometres away.

Wise sheep watch a farmer's hands
for the things that a hand holds,
but the steel nozzle of weed killer

is not food or the promise of food.
Boyle's Law holds and the spray
disperses. The first sheep fall.

Apocalypses are a Christian thing,
whose Book is redolent with
the mythos of shepherds and sheep,

but practising for it is very Buddhist,
and the sheep stop noticing the farmers,
tamed from meditative repetition.

Only a few succumb to the paralysis
of Sarin, the rest keep ruminating,
their wool stained with poison.

The spray works better in the narrow
lungs of a subway station, the toxin
quietly filling the available space.

No saviour ever came to purify
Banjawarn Station. The ragged
sheep wander and grind their black teeth

and the Federal Police arrive late to
snip tufts of fleece, and count the
grinning skulls of the very first martyrs.

I

I've never been happier than at the tennis today, my son and I sitting quietly, posed in our idea of gentlemen, applauding rallies and whispering 'out' or 'in' when Zhang challenged. Three hours and a ball, and the blue Plexicushion. And Show Court 3 in silence. My heart in the final game and I was as excited as the kids I joined at the boundary, holding my sharpie and autograph pad. Alison Riske came to me first. 'Thanks for coming to watch.' 'I love how you fight,' I answered.

Tennis has no time limit. The question, 'When does the match end?' makes no sense. Tennis just goes on. Like other things that are real, there is no limit. Except for the violations. If you have a problem with this, you don't like the good tennis. What is a better question? Why is it so hard to be at the right place at the right time?

The serve is the rhetorical question that I always answered.

To the birds who sing it, song is the aggressive claiming of territory. Australia is home to the world's loudest and most varied songbirds. It is believed that songbirds originated in Australia. It is believed that human song developed in mimicry of birds.

To watch this fight is to be immersed in the distraction. A bird slings by just before serve and is nearly hit by the receiver. My son pulls at his sock and then at his shoe. A ball kid scrapes behind a cricket.

The return is a consequence, it is not an answer. A return is a territorial swoop. There's more juice on the return.

I watched the neighbourhood wash by on the number 1 tram. I closed my eyes and saw Plexicushion blue. This racquet requires tension. More juice. More return.

II

The surface is the most important thing in tennis. The surface
determines the speed and bounce of the ball. The surface determines
the movement of the player coming to hit it.

We would like to show you the
specific steps to a court being
constructed. On site the work

begins. Frequently the
trees and foliage
have to be

removed from the
site. Due to
topography constraints,

excavation and suspension
are often necessary
to level the
playing area

To paint it all is a bit time-consuming. It's not automatic. Obviously.
You can see. It's not done by a machine. So. It's very hands-on. To
resurface the courts every year. To clean them with high pressure.

To then go through a process of three applications on every court.
Every court must be the same. It is all a bit labour-intensive. And speed,
speed is a critical part. Speed is the critical part. Labour is the absolute.
Speed is the absolute.

III

Or depict the Australian terrain. From a high angle, the camera records a scene into which a lone man enters. The commentary box: *déjà vu* all over again.

The man as *arriviste*. The man as case in point. An enigmatic figure that sometimes seems to be working. The man with the miles in his legs.

Flat through the court but a great redirector of the tennis ball, with 40 per cent of his wins against top tenners. He's playing about as well as he can without hitting a cold winner. The problem is, how long can he keep serving like that?

'Close the game! When it's 40 – 30!' At this moment, I write this sentence: Australians are more emotional now.

The court is a discursive space created by finding the first serve. The first game of the second set has taken on a huge significance. The fight is all-consuming. He introduces that drop shot. The errors are coming.

What does it all mean? A complex knowledge that turns on margins, constructed by planners and geographers. This image is structured around a vertical marker and a horizontal marker. Each centres the space. It is an unbelievable exchange. Gestures, numbers, averages, with the existence of general laws. Parity and unity. A taste of soil. A distant land.

I have an exemplary view. I am a cultivated observer.

He wanders onto the court. A topographical parenthesis, or rare, a charismatic Australian.

Describing a way of clairvoyance. The commentary box: I think it's a night we don't dwell on things: life moves on. I take small steps. Then I take a long stride with my foot on this idea.

IV

The Australian Open is on the left-hand television. On the middle
television is a three-minute loop that seems to feature a fitness app. The
right-hand television shows footage of a storm at sea. Then it shows
Manus Island detainees. The right-hand television seems to feature
more events than the television on the left and the television in the
middle. Why have a breakdown every summer? The left-hand television
shows highlights of Nadal's apology to a ball kid. Her face caught a
badly struck ball. I'm fine. I'm quite flushed. The girl is not ready when
Nadal apologises, strokes and kisses her face.

V

Even though it is the longest match he's ever played, we don't watch
Nick Kyrgios win his five-setter. We flick over to Medvedev and Popyrin
and contemplate skinny males instead. Medvedev plays the ball flat
when he wants to, and he knows how to run the back of the court.

What makes this game appealing is that you can be way ahead for
a while. I am conscious of my house, of how it is tidy and quiet and
empty, and is my carpet acrylic? I move around its piles of books. Fake
underarm serve. Followed by the wrecking ball.

VI

I had not read *Letters Home* before. I had not had that kind of phase. My mum is downstairs with the tennis on the television. Or she is sitting somewhere else, waiting for me.

This is wrong of me, maybe. But I like Plath's escalating demands. Especially the way she escalates demands at the end of the book. Somewhere in her last letters she asks if her new sister-in-law, whom she'd never met, might come to England to help with the children. This is an example of how her major problem in life was access to affordable childcare.

In her letters Plath was upbeat until she died. So much of what she wrote was around this conditional: 'if I could only find a girl …' and 'if I can just write uninterrupted for four hours a day'.

That time that family at the ice rink was next to me. The mother listening to her daughter's story, which was a complaint. There was some injustice about permission given or not given and a bathroom or a bathroom door. The mother listened and then discoursed to her daughter about the unhealthy nature of her relationship with her past. 'That's why we don't hold onto things from the past,' she closed.

VII

In the second men's semifinals, there are two beautiful males, *les beaux BOIS*, warming up the court.

After several minutes watching the player profiles, my mother says gravely, 'They're both very good looking.' We were determined to know these beings. This is a totally female principle of gratification, knowing beings. This was our daily work, this agricultural labour, curious all summer to make this surface produce this pulse.

Thoreau said he was determined to know beans—'The Bean-Field' being a pun for 'the being field', this pun alluding to a relation to land set out by the georgic: being guaranteed by turning land to profit. Though he says, 'I was much slower and much more intimate with my beans than usual'. Here is the responsible non-dreamer working only for tropes and commentary in the only open and cultivated field. As I have little experience with this sort of work, there is not yet any commentary.

VIII

And then I say, 'Yeah, mum,' I say, 'I don't even know why I like this tennis.'

It must be mum. When we used to watch it, all those hours. Something to do with Perth summer, the necessary television.

Tennis. I explain how she said she hadn't been watching the Open when I asked her at the airport when I came to pick her up. I met her at the baggage carousel. I talk about how she doesn't remember some of the rules, how she doesn't recognise players, how she doesn't recognise the legends.

I explain that she was a club champion. Hold. I explain that she explained to me how her team just kept winning when they were all teens in the late 1970s. 'We just kept winning,' she said, as great a mystery to her as to anyone else. She couldn't say why they all decided to stop when they reached State. No one could say. One day she placed all her trophies outside.

I raise my left hand. I was born left-handed. I extend it as if to play a chord. Hold.

I can never raise it. No, you can never raise it, you can only be it.

I adore

my sister's sons & **this**

tributary **crow town laughter**

of industry **rhythm   streams**

flow from dense **seedbank sky-**

corridor to ward ancient economies

precious **Gadigal** way

Bidjigal pockets   they're listening

to she-oak **Wangal**

voices regrowing yarns

on occupied **land stored** and spun

along this Wolli **valley walk**   sustaining

familial inflections **accents** rusted

auto- **orchestrations** once

a chain **of mobile ponds &**

from their broken   **long before**

so far from **homelands**

croaking english **grew**

cliff face caves filled

fossil **flood waters** with broken **glass**

wetland salt marsh counterparts

exhaling pan-greenery **& a wound**

a cadenza **remnant filled** this shady **patch**

healing topsoil

tears their properly **good**

ol' holiday **grassroot voices**

all day **sing** memory's out **landish**

creek covered ruins

in love & war

with every light-speckled **lizard**

sipping grevillea dew
or whispers of some such incident
where new growth leaves
sunny pollen on their faces
that would babble like
the Country mind & spring breezes
an image a shady
grove pooled lowest point
a story black magic
(colocasia esculenta)
stemlets tilt &
dance animate in joyful
tangles

Bidjigal Double Brick Dreaming | BROOKE SCOBIE

The smell of Jasmine
Through white fibro walls
Hiding Dad's double brick Dreaming
Pedestal fans wearing dust cardigans
Click click click behind Mum's door
Moaning aircons in lounge room windows
With frames painted shut
Drown out subwoofers
And fully sick burn outs
Two light brown kids
Sunscreen greased and
Melting on summer pavement
Public pool gobstoppers with
Wet paper bags and
Chlorine bleached hair
Cicada shell brooches
Nan's voice kitchen-knife sharp
Through the warm syrup of the day:
Get down off the bloody tree
You'll break your bloody arm

Chicken pocked skin
And oven mitt hands
Turn the dial on
Ancient brown box tellies
Spider web mesh of
Shrieking screen doors
Swing faster than Rottweilers down the road
When they haven't been fed
Biting at your heels
Salting chubby cheeks
Those light brown kids with
Scab adorned knees
Painted with mercurochrome flowers
Stringing buttons on thread
Little fingers pricked with pins and
Mouths full of condensed milk

That'll put proper fat on ya bones
Nan's voice butterfly hushed
Through the brittle chill of the morning:
Don't tell ya bloody mum
She'll wring my bloody neck

The questions two young soldiers asked me
at the King Hussein border crossing checkpoint...

Were you born on a Thursday in Cleopatra
Hospital? Did you come out silently, as day-
break smudged the night sky? And why was
your father absent? What is the name of your
father and his father and his father? Do your
neighbours Mohamed and Faduma water
the orphaned houseplant whenever you are
away? Are you aware your parents first arrived
in Australia with their life savings wrapped in
brown paper, their only English the lyrics to
We are the Champions? Did your mother bring
two dresses, red polka dot and turquoise taffeta,
in her peeling 60s suitcase? Did you correct
her *thanks God?* Did she put up a fight when
you said you were leaving? When he left? And
how was your first Ramadan alone? Did you
miss the walnut maamoul and *Allahu Akbars*
tossed at you Eid mornings? Have you told any-
one about the Enid Blyton books you stole from
Stanmore library, because your mother worked
three jobs? If you flatten your gutturals, is it still
Arabic? Why did your childhood best friend run
away? What man siphoned her dry? Why does
your grief stick to everything? Did inhaling an
onion help with the tear gas they threw during
the protests of '03? What remedies did you inherit
from your ancestors? What skeletons? Who taught
you to roll wara2 3enab like that? Does 2am still
grab you by the throat? Amongst the Gitanes and
sewage and Roman ruins, can Beirut forgive its
people? How many times have you phoned your
mother since? Does your grandmother always boil
her water twice? And why are you still shocked
at how things (don't) work there? What other

city turns its war bunkers into clubs? Its prayers
into curses? And why do the wretched always
sell roses on Bliss street? And how do you revive
the dead? Why did they take your brother? Could
you make out his face amongst the thousands
flickering in the waters of the Mediterranean?
Did he return months after the funeral to ask
you, *what wrongs did I commit?* What village
do you carry on your lips, balance on your
breath? Have you been to Jerusalem during olive
harvest season? Did you pick and press, before the
settlers gathered like acid in your chest and
poisoned the ancient trees? Have you tired yet of
the *may Allah have mercys*? Have they tired of
you? Were you afraid of the men with guns those
nights the power cut? Did you splutter your amens
and sweat out your tasabeeh? Do you remember
the countries you've lost? Do their crooked rivers
still cling to you? Did you hear the aunties, rusted
arms, coarse hairs on chins, call you lonely? Call
you nobody's mama anymore? Did you tell your
mama you named him Omar Al Farouk, after the
revered warrior? Why did it end with your Great Love
Who Changes Everything? Did he make your wide
hips tremble with jazz and derbake? Did he linger
long enough on each letter of *ya leil, ya ein* and
the evening news headlines? Did your hurts trail
behind him like tangled fishing lines, too much for
the life he lived? And does weight like that settle
or lift? And what of the days you feel the earth
greying? And when will you stop writing about borders
and bloodshed and war and death and home? and
home? and home?

To the cities that changed me; inspired by Kaveh Akbar

Breath | EVELYN ARALUEN

J plays the radio in the bathroom, so when the news reports the next death it reverberates across tile and porcelain. They say the fires have grown strong enough to create their own weather systems, to draw down lightning from the smoke. They say they picked a truck up in a tornado of flame and tossed it down a mountain. Last year at the march for Kumanjayi Walker, my nation danced for rain outside Sydney Town Hall. An Uncle told us the ancestors were angry, that they are reminding us what order looks like. Watching the land burn feels like a test of how much I'm willing to see avenged. I run the hotel bath and sit in more water than we're allowed at home, watch my hair swirl in dark tendrils around me. No-one has ever asked, but I'm scared of the sea.

Floating at dawn on the North Atlantic Ocean, I walk the length of the deck as the ferry sways beneath me. I wander as if drunk from lounge to shop to cafeteria. A few passengers are watching the TV absent-mindedly as the newsreader's accent clips unfamiliar over the names of towns that I've walked barefoot, country I've danced and swum and sung. Here where I've slept in slips of morning light, there where we drove wide nights under a river of stars. She calls it a forest fire, and I watch as their mute faces are washed in orange glow. A man leans against the counter where I stand, and I want to say—that's my home, and it's burning. Do you understand how much is alight? That we can't breathe? I watch him watch expressionless before the story changes to the sport and his head tilts, his gaze involved.

I've written poems about fire. I come from a culture of ancient knowledge of and relation with flame. We are each totemically designated through it, our nations are demarcated by our fire stories, by what each terrain needs. It has a place in our body, on the land we pattern with old and new growth to bring that which forages and that which preys. It's our job to know when the wind lifts, when the trees are ready to sigh. There's something intoxicating about air filled with the smoke of burning red gum. Fire breathes and expels air. It knows what to take, if you know what to give it.

I don't know the fire here. It's something to curl around in some building where some old name once took tea. I feel panic rise through me as we pass the pub along the River Liffey, patrons crowding the roaring chimineas while swans honk along the banks. I imagine coals spilling down the cobbled street, the night wailing with sirens. When I check the Fires Near Me app, it opens unmarked somewhere in the British countryside. It's the same notification tone as Dad's emails. We meet cold mornings in home's evening to tallies of the day's carnage, cold fingers scrolling across continents to find our towns. In a groupchat my siblings back home list the roads that are closed each day, sharing screenshots of maps and alerts as if we aren't always already watching, as if by sharing news we already know, we might be able to do something.

It follows us wherever we go. On the radio in the chemist while I'm pondering over candied flavours of fruits that are burning on the branch. In the hotel lobby as we wait to sleep off ten thousand miles. The attendant at the emigration museum who hopes Ireland learns from our mistakes in their next election. The butcher who repeats horrible horrible horrible, the baker who shakes her head for the koalas, the bartender who says that he's sorry as he pours me a cider that tastes like cordial warmed from a southern sun. I run out of synonyms for burning as I watch through a screen, hear my mum's voice strain through my headphones.

Between Sydney, Qatar and Dublin, a clapstick stained with ochre dust goes missing from my luggage. It was carved from a mulga tree at the back of some distantly related uncle's property in Brewarrina, the ochre from veins at the edge of Dharug and Gundungurra country that I gathered on a drive after last year's Hawkesbury NAIDOC. I'm hysterical at its loss, I never wanted to come, I've never wanted to leave home, there are clearly ancestors who don't want me here. What if that tree is gone now? I wail in frantic emails to airport security. What if the fire took it too?

With each day I learn new ways to feel unprepared. Strolling through St Stephen's Green with no words for how to greet the place, no names for the birds. The anxious game of converting currency, the growing ache in my spine, the piercing cold biting at bare ankles. In Oxford I get into a shouting match with an old white man sniggering at a Gamilaroi carving. In London we drag suitcases back and forth through Hyde Park to find the basement we rented cash-in-hand. I don't travel well when all I want is to be home, useless and frightened with ash in my lungs. We sit in Starbucks for three hours as we wait to take our train to Cambridge, reviewing endless pitches to put words to things we are not yet ready to speak: that it's gone too far already, that every year more people will die, that some places will simply never recover. I've already spent a semester marking poetry and prose from students who will probably need to flee their homes in coming years. I've started a book which seeks to tease the icons of Australiana that have been so volatile to this country. They, too, are burning.

We came to talk about temporality, about literature, about the necessity of art in a time of crisis. Whenever I sit to draft remarks, to make a comment, I find myself searching for the balance between sorrow for the living, and willingness for the land to lose us for its own healing. We spent our youths imagining this kind of life, dreaming of ourselves as writers and thinkers who travel the world to tell stories. Being here tastes sour and hollow. This doesn't feel like writing—it feels like relic-making. What use is a poem in a museum of extinct things, where the Anthropocene display is half-finished? I couldn't free the shield, I didn't find the head. What use is witness at the end of worlds?

On Invasion Day, I stand in the stone walls of Cambridge University and the sharp call of Murrawarri mulga rings through the quadrangle. The clapsticks aren't done with me. They come back with new questions: if we are to go, who will care for our relations? Who will greet the trees, who will leave honey for the moon, who will pattern the land with flame?

In Singapore airport J disappears into the smoking room while I stand at our gate, reading a sign advising on health precautions for the virus that has just started to make the news. On the form they ask us to contact a hotline if we experience shortness of breath within fourteen days of our return. In a few months, another black man will die with 'I can't breathe' choked from his throat. We arrive home to a house filled with ash.

beneath our radiant   second verse
   there's more grist for those who
       try to bridge   the great political
          divide
yet
   the ham-fisted   pop-philosophy
tailored to the   silent majority
      slips   into the cracks
& fissures of   this abyss   roughly
   the size of   the desk
      on Q&A   seeping into the drinking water
     like fluoride   to keep our teeth white
         sharp
          & pearly white
   I grip firmly
   to this $7 bottle of wine
that I bought instead of buying groceries
  yelling at the television   on a Monday night
wondering   how many Egyptians died
    building the pyramids
      from the top down
                    where ScoMo sits
            most uncomfortably
     atop that paragon   arrogantly
declaiming us the most successful
   multicultural nation in the world
as if it were an olympic sport
            (tho we all know we'd have
            a better chance of winning
            if it were the comm games)
  looking confused & daggy
 as any politician would getting
actual sand in his boots—it's like
  Napoleon's soldiers shelling off the nose of the sphinx
breathing a collective sigh of relief when
on the back of a dirty postcard a digger writes
post-colonial & doesn't get called up   on it

the sick logic of this being
that   while skin abounds in our sunburnt country being so
sensitive & white   means getting stuck on whether to
stock up or not: choosing vitamin D over aloe vera

girt by increased borders of self-preservation
retreating indoors to complain safely about migration
people wait it out   in suburbs   sparse   & plain

like a buried verse in an anthem
only ever mumbled   by overpaid athletes
words   get lost in their delivery

though it's clear   if Andrew Bolt keeps
talking   & people keep letting him   I don't think
we'll ever be able to   reverse the effects   of such
awful coral bleaching

Conman | DANNY SILVA SOBERANO

On Instagram, I read a screenshot of a Tweet saying,
Can we normalise fucking things up right now?
as if there are people in the world
who are not constantly fucking things up.
I have been a fuck-up more or less my entire life,
right from the moment of birth,
when I came out fully yellow
and not a boy.
Every day I am alive is a mistake.
I am an actively shitty person
every day of my life.
I steal money to pay for narcotics.
I steal narcotics.
I speed on the freeway
and I am the drunkest I have ever been,
a big body bumbling
to survive the deepest part of the night.
I am threatening again
to jump into the nearest river.
On the phone she is begging again
for me to please just drive home.
In another life I please her. Meanwhile,
the rivers are alarmed
by my late night screaming,
incoherent as a fast car.
There are holes I punched
into the walls of houses I never returned to,
people I never saw again.
In messages they say, *You know, D, I forgive you*
just come back. Stay for breakfast in the morning.
I ignore pleas for empathy.
This is not over, they say, and I turn away.
I do not donate the money I am saving
for a cosmetic surgery.
A woman who cares very much for me says,
Every day is not a mistake.
It just doesn't live up to your wild, impossible expectations.

One hundred and fifty dollars, please. Drive home safely.
And please be kind to yourself.
I have conned people into loving me,
I spin plates in the air and they give their affection.
I note every noise of praise and conspire
to accumulate more, only more.
I behave only for praise.
Leave me to embrace my buckets.
I am emptying the river I was born with.
Let the dead bury me where I am found.

The Crayfish | ISABEL PRIOR

Camino de Santiago, June 2019

The river is cathedral cool. Libby wades in
in sports bra and shorts, while I perch on the bank
trying the water like a pair of glass slippers.

Above us, the poplars are a ribbed vault
from which leaves like paper stars peel to press
their faces to the crisp and soundless water

before hissing over washboard rocks downstream.
A crayfish settles atop my foot. My toes
are fat from walking and marzipan pale underwater

and he scales them, proud and proprietorial.
He raises one fleshy pincer, then the other
then he stops short like a matador awed by his own red cape.

We will never be back. Tomorrow we'll shuck
shoes and socks in a new village. We'll stick pins
in virgin blisters and forego towels to dry, sun-spangled,

on another riverbank. Warblers dart by like fish.
Libby backstrokes between them, scattering leaves
that float at once in water and on air,

light as birdsong. The evening is albariño gold
and we've become hushed and reverent, drunk
on sunny silence. We break bread and cheese

and green tomatoes. Libby's flyaways glow green
as she unpicks our water bottles from the wet ankle
of a poplar. When I stand, apricot clouds brush my calves.

For a time, the river is still.
Then, in a flood of sound, the leaves quiver
and the warblers ripple out into the dusk.

creation lament | CLAIRE ALBRECHT

you see the vivid in everything
I see the patina behind my eyelids
you sometimes get asthma
my heart plunks out of tune

swamping my arms through
the smoke for the first time
in four days
I open the recycling bin

and it is just an orgy
of humans, ghosts
and cool green glass bottles
all clinking together like music

and I can't tell if, in all
this, there's a line missing
a counter-melody or the alto like
some crumbled chicken stuffing

or the cork back in your bottle
that keeps it from going off
I mean a something, an extra
that's born from me

and must be kept alive
through smoke, through flood
through fear and the whole
fucking trashfire of it all

and while I suck back a
winfield and a wine I can't
help but wonder if I can't help
this, or another, or anything

resembling a future anymore
not here, not for some new creature
that doesn't want its fur all singed
or an underwater home

even though you and I
hold hands when we fall asleep
in a bad mood even
though we could make a firework

out of this furnace even though
creation could be the only thing
I'm good for - what good is creation
just to watch it gasp for life?

just to lose it? I was born
without doubt, knowing change
and floods and drought would come
and now that they're here—

I want to feel hope like a cloud
growing rain in its belly
and the rampant joy
in its wake, but my fear is unbroken

and barren, and barren, and barren

(crossing my mind) | PAM BROWN

late november apocalypse
mimics
    the black summer
    that began the year

always later than i think
at 4 p m
      outside's still hot as an oven
      have to lie down   (inside)
&
      begin reading the poems
  in a new issue of a magazine

      i try to stay interested
  but that enervates   rapidly

why?

it crosses my mind
that my poetry days
      are probably done

am i done with poems
or
are poems done with me?

more than half a century
    making connections
through strings of words
arranged
not composed
         mostly vertical
&
    often meandering sideways

---

it could be time

---

something   (generative?)
        crossed my mind

i was going to write it down

    walked the short distance
        from the garden doors
(from where i was
watching lines of clumsy bats
echo-lob across an ordinary sunset)
    through our four room house
        to the second room computer

&
couldn't remember it—
        something (generative)

didn't matter

---

last summer
heat stricken bats
fell out of trees to die

we
have devastated
natural environments

    born of immigrants
we've ruined an entire country
in only two hundred & fifty years

i'm sorry for that

---

a compulsion to make poems
        dwindling now

now or nowadays

---

do the bells still ring the hour
      on the Town Hall clock?

the city
      emptied for the pandemic

---

i don't feel
   authorised to say
   i'm the 'author' of my poems

maybe i'm the image
  my poems make of me   (not that)
       or a sign   (not that either)

what does a poet
               <u>do</u>?

---

bright morning sun
verbena creeping   red & green
      along the footpath patch

at the letterbox
      the postie
tells me
she's had a bundle of mail stolen
            from her trolley
'they use it for identity theft'

she hands me a parcel

a paperback,
    i know before i open it
'it's lesley'   i say aloud

'diary of a detour'
lesley stern   she died
        just a few days ago

sorrow
    starts up again

trying to remember
  what book of mine
      did she launch?

can't ask anyone

though
meaghan might remember

no one took any photos

dare not ask

it does seem ridiculous
    to <u>not</u> remember
such a wicked speech
        at gleebooks

(denying my fragility
there are more blanks)

must have been '50-50'
does ken remember?
he published it

Little Esther Books

ken put keanu & river
            on the cover—
cinematic

'dead & alive - the body as a cinematic thing'
        lesley's essay—
                    ten or so years later
began -
        in the cinema many were living
                and many kept on living,
            and many became dead,
            as gertrude stein might say.
some kept on living and some
            kept on being dead
        and some became things ...

---

at dusk i want to climb up
into the huge fig tree on Ashmore Street
        &
        join the clamour of birds
        finding their roosts for the night

---

to begin

another part of a poem

---

hot & bored   on-grid
summer's unusable
crowds everywhere
humid & heavy grey

rub the little scar on my forehead
        want to go back to 1997

just want to
whatever

that was a year of the ox

     we disconnected
       without care

you stayed put

should have
     written back
should have called you
should have done something
     about some things
can't think of what

time is different
time is nothing now

(indifferent now)

   unexpected memories hit
at 2 or 3 a m
     in fractions

why?
decades later?

like this (memory)—

we stacked the poets union meeting
     for equal representation

afterwards
  we smudged the breezy harbour sky
     with marijuana plumes

stoned utopians

---

tonight
so deeply (even more) bored

  political zeal
          on permanent pause

like,
is that 'the real unconscious'
      'the real unconscious & the body'

like,
that's dead?

          is that what happened?

'happens'

---

we went ahead
          &
          made a painting
          of
          the coffee pot
&
  a charcoal drawing
          of a brick

---

we
can't exactly
          name every thing

              'everything'

---

naming the faces
        not knowing the roles

confident
        it's identity-memory that's skewed

---

the only nonentity
        in the village

dreaming i'm reading
then   i'm quoting—

'cementing a position
   as one of the country's leading researchers
with the launch of a first book
                &
                a raft of fellowships & grants'

   'with wry wit   the emperors of the anagram
invent imaginative formal constraints
                        not decor but credence'

alright then   got that
                at 4 a m

---

white white teeth
        ping perfectionist bleats

artist talks
        idling
on the lonesome internet

---

new romantics rusting in the wine bar

---

we began to read
        a few north americans
&
    to copy
        what we called their 'savoir faire'

then
    fanny (author of 'everything's a fake')
        gave the gossip a nickname

                vitamin g

        'come for the vitamin g'

---

when was that?

---

we knew our bodies were political
        as soon as we could crawl

sitting on the floor with me
    you took a small pair of scissors
            from your tote bag
&
slowly
trimmed my fingernails
as desire pumped
        &
            spilled
                all over us

    we made love
we fucked   slept
&
    made love again

we drove in the rain
        to the sea
    into the wind

on the wet sand
you stole a line from me
        for your poem

you knew everything

    you knew
    the hurt filled world
that dragged you
    from your childhood

your cousin was thrown
into the sea to drown

your mother wanted
the medals to be real

it's quiet now

        i've lost
whatever we said

 it's years ago now

    other people
 have asked after you

i don't know where you are

Crowded out | PETER BOYLE

The world presses in,
a towering river of debris glittering
with specks of one on-going explosion.
All of us are morphing,
our faces layered with many faces, two eyes
gazing upward from the ending of time.
Our skin is travelling from country to country
even as we sit still
and the second hand stays
frozen on the wall clock.

From somewhere far inside us
a young woman from a millennium ago
rises to the surface, comes close
and we shiver with all her tenderness.
At the place where our breath is suddenly held back
a child is there, watching the trees above him
spin in fast motion. In the vast
empty bar room of the mind
a skeleton holding a wineglass
gives us a familiar nod.
Birds fly in and out
of the multiple cages
that are our rib cage.
A single cry from any one of their throats
is enough to thread
white light across the darkness.

So large, so impossible—
our hands shake
as we carry the world.

The dilemma of writing a poem without light,
without the amenities of paper and ink
Without the digital keyboard
But with memory correcting each verse
Like a clock tired of telling the time,
a fallen rhythm into language
in the calm of the dawn.
Only then, re-reading it
from the blue caressing
the dew on the glass in my window.
Only printing it in the flight
of the last waking dream.

Don't Call Us Dirty | LOU GARCIA-DOLNIK

The speaker loves their mother from a distance although,
anxious at the prospect of having no-one to dedicate this poem to
misdiagnoses several of her cohabiting morbidities
and tries to solve everything with lesbianism.

Circle the same green city where everything is imbued
with the scent of decay, everybody dating each other
crying about time, unable to make sense of emotional liberalism
though this doesn't stop lovers from telling her *you're too much*
you hurt me, but I got over it. that's white-adjacent queerness
she shrugs: shotgun gay wedding through life   the bioregion
her racial constitution in some stranger's mouth a precursor
to netflix and fucking

attracting detritus with her longing for something other
than the armageddon of malignant havingfeelings,
she spends eons distilling an essential truth
from the platitudes of terminal desire i.e.
              you're unlovable   too heavy
              never as new as the other girl

& those were the halcyon days of thievingthievingthieving
living in anyone else's ugly histories, as in
baby, i love you   i can't do this tonight
i was thinking about her so much i couldn't get wet

following her cartographic impulse, maps human relations
with generous humour
tells every butch   *you can be my father*
every femme   *i can be your mother*
anyone in-between   *we could be together forever*
genuflecting to the subject of her idolatry
and throwing it all away with
                         you don't care about me enough

though if she ever made light of nights wasted in allyship with ugly haircuts
it wasn't difficult to forget her own genealogy was a hierarchical one
its holy triptych the sun   a marred childhood   the state
beating down on bodies looking to eschew the cargo of an oath
to feeling unfree

tells lovers *do not save me*   self-sufficiency a drug
running through the veins of chronic loneliness
holding tight to the mantle of her blamelessness
anyone's arms corrugated bars through which the sky
cast shadows over the origins of her affliction

in worship of the catastrophe of love on lockdown
lawlessly, this desire to be dirtied where living
ran the body unclean   commands daily a plea
to god in the machination of every fresh heartbreak:

I permit myself to pray at this temple
I permit myself to take refuse in it

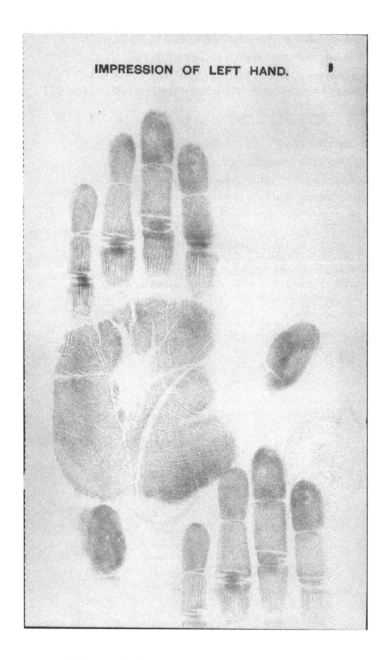

Image of Bhouta Khan's hand, 7 July 1916, author's great-grandfather

i.
Immigration Restriction Act 1901
[Being the Matter of Bhouta Khan]

we certify on this day
the examination of the alien
to the *Nation*—Mr Bhouta Khan
& grant him permission to land
if he is able to show he is/or one or another of:

>
> a *bona fide* naturalized citizen of Australia holder of
> Certificate No. ...
>
> (or)
>
> that he was born in Australia in the state of ...
>
> (or)
>
> that he is the *bona fide* holder of Passport No. ...

NOTE: we must strike out all reasons for his entry to our lands except
that on which landing is allowed, which may not include marriage to
a *natural born* Australian; which may not include love; which may not
include human decency; which may not include reasons that Mr Bhouta
Khan is a *true man*.

ADDITIONALLY NOTE: the handprints of Bhouta Khan, both left
& right are on the back hereof, along with photographic evidence, both
portrait & left & right profile.

ii.

TESTIMONY (presented to THE COLLECTOR H.M.
CUSTOMS), Flinders Street, Melbourne, on the 26th day of June
1916)

I am Bhouta Khan, of 124 Young Street, Fitzroy & I beg to apply for a
Certificate of Exception under the *Immigration Restriction Act 1901*,
Section 4 (n) to visit the country of India for a period of six months
with my immediate family. On solemn oath I undertake that I shall
not return to Australia any relative, expired, revoked, of dark skin,
dark eyes, foreign tongue or pagan habits, peculiar dress sense, exotic
produce or accompanying animals, *livestock or wild*. I attach three
character references & six unmounted photographs—three full face,
three profile.

Self-attesting to my good character, please allow me to state that this
day on the 24 June 1916 I arose from bed & went into the bathroom
to shave. In the cracked mirror I saw a human being. I sat at the table
in the kitchen with my wife & child. We breathed together & we ate a
meal together. I then went to the washhouse at the rear of the property
& bathed my dark skin with disinfectant for some time. When I was
satisfied that I had cleansed my physical body to the standard you
require (Regulation 16, Section 2) I bathed a second time. Without
your permission, my wife kissed my right cheek before I left the house
for the working day. In the street I greeted neighbours with a discreet
nod of the head & they returned the gesture, with the exception of the
butcher on the nearest street corner who cordially addresses me as
nigger each morning. I hold no malice toward him as I have not been
granted permission by your department to do so. During my working
day, selling haberdashery and supplementary goods door-to-door in
several neighbourhoods, I smiled regularly & I robbed no one. I did not
look upon a white woman's body & when asked, I agreed that *yes*, I was
fortunate to be allowed to reside in such a fair and prosperous *Nation*.
That evening I again sat with my wife & child, I again bathed & my wife
& I shared the same bed.

If my application to travel is granted & if I am in fact allowed to return to this fine country without displaying a proficiency of language— Mandarin—please intimate the fact to me at the above address; Yours Faithfully, Mr Bhouta Khan.

ADDITIONALLY NOTE: the handprints of Bhouta Khan, both left & right are on the back hereof, along with photographic evidence, both portrait & left & right profile.

iii.
Book No. 201
Form No. 21
<u>**Duplicate:**</u> **No. 071**
Certificate Exempting From Dictation Test

I, Percy Whitton, the Collector of Customs, being
Percy, a benevolent man, Percy, an upstanding
Christian, Percy of the Order of Freemasons,
Percy, descendent of Pioneers, hereby certify
that Mr Bhouta Khan, who claims to be a man,
be granted permission to be exempt from the
Immigration Act (1901–1912) for a period of three years.

To be certain that the Bhouta Khan who leaves
this land is the same Bhouta who returns I submit to
the Commonwealth the following description of him:

Nationality: Indian
Age: 52 years
Height: 5 feet 7 inches
Build: workhorse
Complexion: dusky as sunset
Eyes: unknowable
Religion: unspeakable

ADDITIONALLY NOTE: the handprints of Bhouta Khan, both left
& right are on the back hereof, along with photographic evidence, both
portrait & left & right profile.

iv.

STATUTORY DECLARATION — COMMONWEALTH OF AUSTRALA

I, Bhouta Khan, Hawker, residing, living, being at
do solemnly & sincerely declare, defer, etc., etc.,
I was born in *British India* to *British India* for the
benefit of *British India* at Gurmalla in the year 1864
& sailed to the *British Colony* of Victoria in 1896 where
I now reside. I also solemnly declare that upon entering
the colony, the *Nation*—the fine Australian *Nation*—
was not in existence. I therefore additionally declare that
I cannot be subject to a *Nation* that was an aberration
not only in my mind, but in that of your founding fathers.
Additionally, therefore, I claim that I should be subject to
regulations, sub-sections & paragraphs (etc.) adjudicated
within the legal framework of Britain, not Australia, as the
Empire covets for Eternity, *Her* global colonies.

>   I declare this statement at: Melbourne, Victoria
>   on the 26th day of June 1916 before a:
>   *Police; Special; or Stipendiary Magistrate; a Justice of*
>   *The Peace; a Commissioner of Affidavits; or a Commissioner*
>   *For Declarations Dog Licences & Fines*—with the full
>   knowledge that in making a false statement—in
>   particular any statement
>   that sullies the *Nation*—that I will become liable
>   to imprisonment, with or without hard labour
>   (& possibly both), for a period of … years.

ADDITIONALLY NOTE: the handprints of Bhouta Khan, both left
& right are on the back hereof, along with photographic evidence, both
portrait & left & right profile.

v.
Customs and Excise Office
3 July 1916
<u>**Memorandum:**</u>
To the Officer-in-Charge of Police

In order for the Commonwealth to accept
photographs of Mr Bhouta (Khan) in evidence
the following procedures must be followed:

>applicant Khan should be seen, physically,
>& compared to image held of him
>by Customs, in grey metal filing cabinet
>(alongside the oven) in staff kitchen

>the photograph in the filing cabinet
>must be shown by Officer to persons
>providing certificates of character of (Khan)
>(alongside the oven) in the staff kitchen

>whether applicant (Khan) is known or unknown
>or a known-unknown, police must arrange
>an interview with those providing certificates
>(alongside the oven) in the staff kitchen

>so that there be no doubt etc. as to the
>identity of person under discussion (Khan)
>the photograph must also be sworn under oath
>(alongside the oven) in the staff kitchen

>if reason is to be provided that the applicant (Khan)
>is known to the police for any reason whatsoever
>he will be denied an Exemption Certificate
>(alongside the oven) in the staff kitchen

ADDITIONALLY NOTE: the handprints of Bhouta Khan, both left & right
are on the back hereof, along with photographic evidence, both portrait & left
& right profile.

vi.

Report by Police Officer on/within Exemption Applications

I, Senior Constable Cliff Hitchings, have made enquiries & interviewed the applicant, Boota Khan. (Khan insists that his name be spelled as B.H.O.U.T.A., but having made additional enquiries, I note that on the original shipping document when Khan arrived in the Colony of Victoria, Immigration Officers gave preference to the spelling B.O.O.T.A. The phonetic generally suffices with foreign names & I have chosen to adopt such an approach here.) Khan states that he has resided in the *Nation* for seventeen years & that his occupation is a Hawker. The attached photographs appear to be that of the applicant, but I would suggest they & Khan both be examined by a forensic scientist, as his own skin appears to be several shades lighter than the Boota Khan of the photographs. The attached testimonies attest that Khan is a man of sober character & a decent man, a good man, a *true man*. Not a white man, but a man nonetheless. To ascertain if the Boota Khan who presented himself to this office on this day is the same Boota Khan in the photographic images in addition to being the same Boota Khan discussed in the attached testimonies, I brought *my* Boota Khan before those citizens of Australia who had made representation on his behalf. It was agreed between myself & the two gentlemen concerned that the Boota Khan in our presence, the Boota Khan of six photographic images (three full front & three in profile) & the Boota Khan of sober character, is the same person. (Khan did not dispute our findings). I therefore recommend that the photographs, the testimonies and the existence of Boota Khan be accepted as fact (in triplicate).

ADDITIONALLY NOTE: the handprints of Bhouta Khan, both left & right are on the back hereof, along with photographic evidence, both portrait & left & right profile.

vii.
Testimony provided by Latoof & Callil
Importers of Fancy Goods
262–4 Exhibition Street, Melbourne
16th June 1916

We wish herein to humbly certify
that we have known Bhouta Khan
for something like fifteen years.
Khan is honest, Khan is industrious,
Khan bathes regularly (in fact, several
times per day we are led to believe).
Khan keeps to himself with the exception
of providing occasional polite discourse
on matters excluding politics.
He defers, he looks a man in the eye
with due deference and respect.
We conclude that Khan is harmless
and therefore, no harm should come to him—
for now.

ADDITIONALLY NOTE: the handprints of Bhouta Khan, both left
& right are on the back hereof, along with photographic evidence, both
portrait & left & right profile.

viii.
Testimony provided by J.H. Pritchard,
'Elsa', 14 Denmark Street, Kew

etc. etc. etc. etc. etc. etc. etc.
Boota [sic] Khan of Young Street
Fitzroy for eighteen years—a Hawker is:

> Honest
> Sober
> Law-abiding
> Reputable
> Loyal

'Boota Khan has never been any trouble to me
He has never been any trouble to us
He will never be any trouble to the *Nation*
Boota Khan may well be a man—as is his claim—
But he will never be a man of trouble'

ADDITIONALLY NOTE: the handprints of Bhouta Khan, both left
& right are on the back hereof, along with photographic evidence both
portrait & left & right profile.

There are exactly 12 eggs
in a dozen; the exact number of nuts you
should eat per day. 1 can be considered exact, even tho
the ancients didn't think it a number. Exact numbers are got
by counting, but not by "measuring". 9,999,999 is
an exact number. So is 6, 7, 8, and 772.
To return: return # T if the number Z is returned,
otherwise # F exactly. 12 tables in a restaurant, is exact, but
if you see 8 tables, you may wonder; lies without
number. Exact numbers, when it comes down to counting
the number of dead, and injured on a battlefield
may be disputed. Write down the exact amount, if you're
that good. Sentences with "exact amounts of
cash" are popular. Find the exact number, for each situation.
"4" is the largest exact number a kid under 5 knows.
Exact numbers aren't hard to copy. Matching up
all the digits in an exact number, is imperative. There are 30
synonyms for *inexact*, including: false, inaccurate,
ambiguous, and imprecise. Exact (*strictly* accurate),
Inexact (*strictly* No). 7.2 chairs is an exact number, but
2.1 children isn't. Beware of getting involved with
inexact numbers, even if they give you better results. (They
may not mean what you think they mean). A very large
inexact, is not the same as a very small one.
3% may be the exact value, but just not close enough;
an exact number, may (silently) return an inexact
number, nevertheless. You can be thinking inexactly, but
turn up nevertheless exactly. An inexact shape
might be exactly, what you went out looking for.
An inexact expression, can be
          quite a thought.

Exoskeletons | JOHN KINSELLA

Words are less inherently
appealing less appealing
inherently only as skin
needing to graft extra
senses though likely that's
too harsh an abrasive rub
of wild oats and seed spikes

through socks wandering
the routes of machine
to home-usage, chains
of command that take and give
but mainly take, all falling
before the trimmer cable
flayed out of speech;

The whole frame shudders
and vibrates though
fingers don't ease the ache
of hinges, to work
with or against the gradient
is semantics
for micro-climates;

A metal eyelet lost on
a hillside enacts self-
protection to deport
as raw material and not object
as commodity one step
closer to origins & answer.
I search futility.

Walking a steep incline
friendship is never closer
or further than slipping
back into one's own foot-
marks; holds let go

one by one as subject-tracing
a journey that can't begin.

All of the seed falling
and so much needed &
unwanted, the scattering
of figuratives to make
greenhouses of silos
rather than places of
storage, contra-excursives.

It's like that turning
of year at higher revolutions,
that fling of covers—
similes were invented as
a way in or way out, a relief
or substitute from labour.
Cuts, callouses, a trapdoor

spider pulling back down
as I approach, but I—
you—we—will go 'round
its circuit, its ambit
and orbit, its influence
where crossing-over is
to be stung and dragged down,

dissolved and supped on.
Exoskeletons—invertebrate
refrain till the interior
pushed back into light
collapses and compresses,
which is the powerhouse
of geo and orbit

via a state of health
to reclaim body or soul
and yet let go of that claim
on first-aid or medicaments,
exercising rights of
passage and abode as
substitutes for conscience.

eyelashes | MELINDA SMITH

She remembers Matt-from-down-the-road. She remembers his uncle's panel-van, parked on the street in front of his house; the car body's dull red, the rust-spots on the driver's door. Remembers sitting talking to Matt in the back of the van; its brown carpet, its wet-dog, engine-oil smell. Remembers the uncle crossing the yard, hopping into the van, sitting cross-legged in ripped jeans, lighting up a Winfield Blue; his white-blond hair, his white eyelashes, almost invisible; him chatting, asking questions. She does not remember crossing her own legs, her shorts gaping, showing candy-striped underpants. She does remember the uncle reaching out, his jabbing finger, him slipping it inside the fabric, deft, practised. Him grinning *better not sit like that, or that's what'll happen* Her face hot, then cold; Matt and the uncle giggling; her dizziness; her silently-closing legs; her sense that around her there had descended a small fug of shame. She remembers that dull red feeling, its stink of engine oil, wet dog, Winfield Blues. Does not remember how many years it stayed.

I am here
Ngatha
I am from
This country
Ngathajungu barna
This barna
Ngatha Barnagu

There are no fucken surprises
During COVID-19 here in
Geraldton on Yamaji barna
The lines on the maps
Were drawn long ago
6pm Curfews—reserve segregation
Markings on the ground known

A mask on our face is not
A tape over our mouths
We cannot be silenced
BLM Stop Black Deaths in Custody
BLM Justice for Ms Clarke …RIP
BLM Justice for Ms Dhu …RIP
Colonial hate remains the killer

I am here
Ngatha
I am from
This country
Ngathajungu barna
This barna
Ngatha Barnagu

I get fidgety standing on
retail floor line markings
The looks of annoyance
The looks of disbelief
Oops that white multhu

Gave me a dirty look
For standing too close

Covid-19 did not stop the
racist online violence here in
My community where they
Still post in cyber blood on
Geraldton Neighbourhood Watch
With keyboard fingers oozing hate
They want to kill us Yamaji

I am here
Ngatha
I am from
This country
Ngathajungu barna
This barna
Ngatha Barnagu
Ground markings for thousand years
Memory into Yamaji DNA to carry
Onwards and forward into time
Survival instinct of our Elders
1905 Act experiences and stories
Bush life Station life shared in yarns
Teachings passed on giving strength

While the others stressed about
Toilet paper to wipe their backsides
The White Australia wheel rolled on
Over us adding extra layers of trauma
Suicides in parks, prisons, communities
Cyber bullying of our young ones
A pandemic stopped nothing in WA

I am here
Ngatha
I am from

This country
Ngathajungu barna
This barna
Ngatha Barnagu

Some Elders said "we be right"
Remember many Ancestors survived
The Pandemic of Colonisation
Segregation is good for us in 2020

Family are like rocks | SHIRLEY KNGWARRAYE TURNER

Family are like rocks | sometimes you want
to throw them out | and some you want
to keep | but you can't | because they're still
falling back | rolling back | like a marble
Family are like rocks | you can pick them up |
and some rocks | never want to be picked up |
because some rocks just want | to lay around and
don't want to learn | they just want to feel sorry
for themselves | family | like rocks | some rocks
become gold | some rocks stay coal
Yes sometimes we have to hold a rock | because
we can't leave them behind | they are precious
to us | and we love our family | forever | no
matter what | we all belong to big hills and
mountains | that made us all rock | and stone |
in the end | we are rocks | all gathered | together

to search for the source
of extraction in expression
      while economies collapse
over breakfast and Brecht
      isn't here to Instagram
his Weißwurst in the sands
of Byron Bay where 5G conspiracies
      radiate foaming breakers
      into COVID tanks
moaning like air being conditioned
out the back of a Dan Murphy's
      and the sexuality
of machinery in its lust
      for extinctions that anti-creation
search for bliss cum and oil warm
      and thick dropping onto the stomach
of our anthropocentrism where we
is a producer of I solutions
jogging in city parks feeding the realisation
that all fictions now can be refracted
      into facts as all frictions struggle
to depict truth as an act
      listening now
      as a baby cries to Nepalese singing
soothing the air above Sydney the morning
      an ibis smudged so brown
it's as if it was used to sweep
      the chimney of a Victorian terrace
where Tibetan flags hang above a sign
that attempts to

STOP
COAL
SEAM
GAS

and perhaps
all one needs is a dream of the west
as a mosquito on earth's arms
seeing how much it can suck
before being whacked
and so to be a bird of thought
edited by nothing but sun
in a Pleistocene memory of ice
melting revealing sandstone cliffs
that form valleys of ironbark
and eucalypt rivers that flood
down escarpments to shape
South Pacific estuaries
how all these ideas are just volcanic
magma in the feet of water
watching two magpies circle and descend
dropping like an absence of rain
into the shower's bucket
startling the hair clip of a dragonfly
hanging from a bush of hair
its bright red tail denser than any
word-colour suggests
dipping its tail in a clear forest pool
cool on a 40-degree day
as you lay back into a place
where words are like kelp
tossed beneath a wave
sequestering carbon
for a reparative state

18 May 2018

Flight 972 crashed at 12:08 p.m., less than 30 seconds after take-off. It immediately banked sharply to its port side over an open paddock.

Ten pastors and their wives from Havana's Church of the Nazarene were among the 113 passengers and crew that lifted off in a 39-year-old Boeing 737-201 ADV from Santiago de las Vegas Airport, Cuba. Damojh LLC of Mexico City was the aircraft's fifth owner, subleasing the asset to Global Air that subsequently hired it out to Cubana de Aviación for charter service. It was forbidden to enter US or Canadian airspace.

The flight recording began with cabin crew laughter and chatter about their previous night out. The pilot gave vessel command to the co-pilot who was on his first service after a 5-year hiatus without interim training or practice.

'What did this guy do?' the captain is recorded. He took command of the craft, heaved the wheel to the left and righted the aircraft for three seconds. Banking occurred five times, each more violently. The aircraft pitched upwards, inverted, dropped, collided with a herd of dairy cattle, struck a farmhouse and then disintegrated along a railway line just as its twin engines were reaching maximum thrust with zero response from guidance systems. Four passengers survived the impact, with two living less than a week. Grettel Landrove, age 23, lived another 31 days.

Mailén Díaz Almaguer, age 19, found wrapped around twisted rail line, was immediately transferred to Calixto García Hospital where she spent the next 205 days. She did not have respiratory, pulmonary, urinary or digestive function on arrival and suffered paraplegic nerve damage. Additional injuries noted included disfiguration of the spine, cervical collapse, compressed thoracic dorsal extremities, splintered tibia, fibula and pelvis, and gluteal burns that required constant draining.

An investigative committee found that the actual take-off weight far exceeded what was recorded and used in pre-flight calculations. The aircraft's centre of gravity was 10% further astern than what crew believed, exacerbating incorrect weight ratios to 29% greater than accounted. Extreme banking would have caused enough centripetal force to pull passengers off seats.

On her 20th birthday in December 2018, Mailén resumed social media by posting her first post-accident selfie on Facebook. Lenier Mesa, Cuban popstar, paid her a surprise hospital visit, presenting her with a statuette of St. Francis of Assisi, patron saint of animals and environment, and a plush toy cow.

When a Yellowstone National Park ranger crew returned the next day, they discovered that Colin Nathaniel Scott, age 23 of Portland, Oregon, had completely dissolved.

Wyoming's Norris Geyser Basin is the hottest, most active geothermal region in the park. Water temperature ranges from 80-237°C. Geysers are fed by underground water enriched with the sulphuric acid produced by green, orange and lavender-coloured microorganisms that break down hydrogen sulphide found in rocks and soil. They ascend thermal currents to pool surfaces and cluster in pastel streaks with a pH value of 1.

Colin and his younger sister, Sable, breached a protected boardwalk and hiked 200 metres to bathe in thermal water, colloquially known as hot-potting. Sable began filming her brother as he reached down to check the temperature of a pool two metres wide, four metres deep and what turned out to be 92°C. She captured Colin slipping and falling into the acid bath.

Calcified minerals rimming the pool were too brittle to assist him. Sable ran to the emergency phone at Porkchop Geyser to summon West District ranger Tara Ross, who responded immediately. All geysers are enclosed. Hazard signage is visible from hiking trails, car parks and feature on billboards throughout Yellowstone. Warnings appear on park-issued maps and are discussed in person as you enter the park.

Once Colin's apparel disintegrated, he went into immediate shock, with extreme universal pain. His nervous system no longer registered sensation after one minute. His epidermis, dermis and subcutis layers eroded completely. Capillaries burst with full blood loss, muscle tissue terminated function and all subcutaneous fat boiled off. Universal organ failure occurred. Colin's skeletal structure fractured, and his bones began breaking down in the swirl of acidic solution. Sable resumed filming.

An emergency crew led by Deputy Chief Ranger Lorant Veress staged numerous attempts to enmesh Colin's remains from the hotpot's opaque water with long catch poles, but the location was precarious and a lightning storm was gathering. Recovery was suspended until dawn.

What remained of Colin was a melted orange flip-flop and a blackened wallet containing driver, hunting and fishing licenses and a retailer rewards card. The ASTM International Resin Identification Coding System lists the type of rubber used in the flip-flop's manufacture as 7—a durable polymer that cannot be recycled.

Years ago I worked at a furniture factory. Some people would say (then and now) that a person who read books all the time would be better off working at a library. 'It's all trees', I'd say to them. Being the hirer and firer got me my nickname. I'm not sure if mine came first, or Fairytale's. The foreman earned that one. We were on and off for most of the time I worked there. He would come home with lipstick in his pocket, porridge in his mo, spinning some yarn about having his tyres stolen. If there were layoffs I always got Fairytale to give the crew a little speech at smoko. First he'd mention the bosses, then the law, then the government, then the unions, then the trees, and by the time he got to the koalas they just wanted to know who was getting the boot and not why. I was learning to sing 'Fairytale' with the town choir for the annual town-founding celebrations. There was no ideological point to it. But then the Pointer Sisters nicknames started to spread. Should I Do It (shortened to Should) and Jump (For My Love (mostly just Jump)) were brother and sister, and the song titles seemed to sum up their dispositions and relationship. Automatic drove an automatic, but once we dubbed them that everything else they did (and said) seemed "automatic". So far so literal, but in traditional reverse style Slow Hand (Slow) was the fastest worker we had, and would sometimes make elaborate sculptures out of the wood, disassembling an elephant with an umbrella and reassembling it as a patio bench, in the same time it took someone else to just do the latter. He's So Shy (Shy) was known for pissing in public, and general exhibitionism. We tried (I'm So) Excited (first Excited, then I'm, then So) on the secretaries, thinking it might help them be enthusiastic, but it was the kiss of death. After the second quit, we learned our lesson and used it on the dourest person in the place. In retrospect it was a bit rough, but they stuck around. Still called Excited even though retired to the Sunshine Coast, I've heard. They were the greatest hits, the best of, there were dozens of others I had to wrangle on paper every day, and then go home and do the same with Fairytale in person at night. You'd think my name would make me unpopular, but actually the crew used it as an excuse to come up close to me on frosty mornings, rubbing their hands. I guess you can't stop romanticism. And no, we never had an actual fire—I was in charge of workplace safety too. This, as I said, is too long ago, and telling you is how I forget.

Flight paths | LOUISE CRISP

(Yellow-bellied Glider *Petaurus australis*)

Blind as a colonial

1. Roaring Mag

A glide between two knolls on Roaring Mag Ridge above the Mitchell—
swooping through White Stringybark, Ironbark and Silvertop 30 degrees
to the horizontal and considerable manoeuvrability turning 180 degrees
in mid air from the fifth finger to the ankle across country 100m at a time
to the Apple Box sap-feed trees on Baldhills Track scheduled for burning
Warm evening in summer a light breeze sufficient to stir leaves at midnight

2. Watts Creek

A glider road travels east-west across the low plateau of the foothills
from the remnant patch of bush on private land to the rough track
between tributaries of Watts Creek the last stand of old hollow trees
hosting dens to thread through young forest picked over 50 years ago
to the grove of Apple Box trees windward the cold wind in winter
is turned aside by the rising land & furrowed Ironbarks along the border

3. Wattle Creek

A network of glide paths on the western fall down to Wattle Creek
from the knoll on Harding Road the deeply scored Apple Box sap trees
are red with frequent use and almost dying from the encircling incisions
Gentled by unburnt open country Velvet-bush and *Pomaderris* near
to flower I cross diagonal towards the sap trees at the washed out ford
the escarpment chittering with swift parrots in the flowering Red Box

4. Stony Creek

Flogged and *hammered* the lowland forest for decades repeatedly
burned and logged the narrow verdant strip along Stony Creek
a haven for Wonga Pigeon, Whipbirds and Tufted Honeyeaters
tall Mountain Grey Gums shade the sandstone slabs & shallow pools
Above the creek flat a few Apple Box sap-feed trees gather in a village
of gliders approached via a flight path un-countenanced before any burn

5. Harding Track

The scars on the Apple Box tree on the hill are grey and calloused over
within a glide of the old-growth forest along Stony Creek clear-felled
to the edge of water—Harding Track runs east past stumps large enough
to stand two men legs apart to balance a chainsaw against the slope
Oval shadows mark the entry to hollows in two Mountain Grey Gums
left standing beside the track the rest of the hillside is silenced voiding
the flight path uphill from here—never to make it back to the ridgeline

circulate this amongst your friends critical of the local culture
at lambing flat. without a public right, british settler methods
of housekeeping have always been cheerful

and patiently ~~endured~~ insured in history symposia, where the dirt
and squalor of anti-chinese agitation is re-tweeted in 140 characters
or less alongside women's rights,

car insurance, and most fervently, the lack of gluten-free options
in dining establishments. the chief mandarins from our country
are cooks, storekeepers and irrigation experts

who know that to enjoy good health in this hot climate of australian
national identity, (which does not exclude fish-curing germans, swedes
or danes) we must at all times

be congenial domestic servants, never loafing about, never liquored.
on arrival we must declare our offspring, our nest eggs, our avian
influenzas

and submit repeatedly to the neurosurgeon's interrogation: *do your
synapses fire loyally?* in little bourke street we ~~gamble~~ ramble
sober, assiduous, apt and docile.

throughout the commonwealth the music of harps does not obscure
their indefatigable legislations. what vigilance. every night they watch
us paddling upstream in junks,

picking up dead dogs for supper. in these dark waters we are stoic:
starving, stealing and vanishing our own sentences: yes sir, all light
sir (mister dead ghost man).

on saturdays the sychophants among us can be seen out cycling
on floating red gum floors and buying twopenny packets of opium
for sale in public offices.

sundays are spent in petting zoos [open season all year]. we are
(*chortle*) ducks, cooked in pots branded ALL-MEN-ARE-EQUAL
(*can't tell 'em apart, gladys*)

amid the yellow-face lacerations we hear only "*ni hao… maaate—
can't you take a joke?*" the western market is glutted with the art
of printing, gunpowder, the mariner's compass.

Note. This poem includes phrases borrowed and derived from: L. Kong Meng, Cheok
Hong Cheong, Louis Ah Mouy, eds. *The Chinese Question in Australia*, 1878-79.
Melbourne: FF Bailliere. 1879.

Ghazal For Shame | *JANIRU LIYANAGE*

My lover's hands were a metaphor for a face with nothing but a mouth and I spent all summer pouring
inside it; nailed to its night, I circled frame after frame. Against each rifle, I pushed my mud-greyed eyes.

I bucked. I begged, I balmed my tongue in compass oil. Now, my father's mother,
cyst-saddled brain, flickers under all my poems; each one, a smoke-braid eye.

At the altar, my blood gathered in thick crowns around my neck. Every streak, a broken voice
lilting into the night, begging, *I will not end. I will not end this poem on shame.* Stay. Eye

the sheened myth of my body. Eye my most feathered limbs. In the airport, the border patrol
agent searches for my quietest parts. Hand down my throat, he laughs; pulls teeth; flays eyes

into a kind of technology, or a kind of echo. *Your english is very good, it's almost like you were born here.* Listen, if to
drown means to be swallowed, I am always drowning inside my country. It took me years before I could say "I"

in a poem. Now, how to stop? In a dream, my village is burning and my god has no face
and only fire. Strange, how the guards use dying light to muzzle the stowaway's eyes.

Yes, I can bay your english—its shine stung ruddy in my fists. Janiru, stupid boy, tidy slaughter of ghosts;
say what you will. Wild as you must, but here's a mirror. Here's a field where every word means *open.* Lie.

Ghost Song (Melbourne 2020) | JONATHAN DUNK

Thought is a cancer of time: the heavens die in their
orbits, bored of revelation, but our stubborn bricks
cling to the dead utopias of pornographic day. Take
this bread of quilted mornings and nail it to the ironic
streetlights. Let our shutterstock houses to wonder
where the ghosts went. Uber dead gods to bet against
addiction. Spend three days sober and rise again:
obsession is honest, and Marx lacks false consolation.
Read John Forbes: *the truth that doesn't set us free*. Ghosts
are economies of scale and three days is too long to be
awake. Take this pill and follow it to the belly of a
whale, don't pray, but wake to whichever sun scalps
the waiting-room wall. Reddit will mutter that a
helicopter circles your favourite suburb, take the
difference on the echo of faith: this city is a desert,
and time stops in each day. Our state regulated faces
are rimed with coal dust and *thc* as we drift and snag
on thickets of twisting metal. If you think about it
you'll wake into or from dissociation on a street of
citric Californian bungalows and children-less bikes.
Scrawled chalk minerals will invite you to stand and
count for something and the angels in their crass
and violent splendour will mockingly demand your papers.
Who among us can claim to be essential with a straight
face. Twilight is more often and abruptly broken, most
songs will be the end of something at dawn. Satan has
room for compassionate grounds and the roadbeds
will be cool and clear as fatuous clouds fondle their
chemtrails. Descartes had trouble with daemons
pulling levers: *I shall consider myself as not having hands or
eyes, or flesh, but as believing I have these things*. But mine
and I are cell mates: don't moralize—delusions can be
tender but the paranoid fuck missed the point because
the real killer will be time, and he should have written
I think that I've thought that I've thought that I've
thought and repeat when it hurts. Corvid songbirds
have souls unfortunately: mania can be a dance

but for months the catastrophe stumbles on without glamour: I is an it and it's all there is, your lovers are shopping lists. We come to dawn to speak with the dead, and in a catacomb of curfewed streetlights you meet the shadow of an intimate stranger, and break guilt with them nailed on empty streets like Christ's thieves, and which of us is penitent depends on no-one looking. The implausible shapes of our ghosts riot and chant in the streets, see them trading lacrimal glands, waving the holes in their wrists, and moving their lips when they talk. Behold our industrial saints with negatively geared halos filigreed in Yves Klein lithium. Our funereal billionaires will outlive the sun. Let the dead bury the dead, someone must.

Glossary for Our Women | *MUNIRA TABASSUM AHMED*

	SKIN	HOMELAND	GOLD	BODY
MEANING	warm brown earth turning over // end of the rainy season	বাংলাদেশ // the space where we were planted	sunlight passed down from wrist to wrist // translated: "a gift for you"	the aperture that our ancestors inherit
SYNONYMS	truth, motion // growth, carambola see also: gold, body	lychee flesh, blood spilt for a language see also: body	honey, spark, summer see also: skin, stolen	the first incision into a lychee's skin see also: homeland
ANTONYMS	paint, mimicry, false body	rewritten memories; burnt histories // colonised bodies	glass, temporary	ego, land lying fallow, cheap mockery
GREAT LOVES	healing; sweetness // slowness	birdsong, mustard oil, storytelling	the shape of a jhumka // the chiming of small bells	celebration // Brown Joy

guided meditation ASMR— your therapist's intern calms you down roleplay — monotonous colonial apocalypse comfort ASMR #RoadTo100K | ALISON WHITTAKER

I know obviously you've got stuff going on, but please get up. They don't really pay me for this, it's a cadetship.

Okay, well, since you're gonna lie prostrate on the floor like that I mo'aswell practice. Can I join you? Any objections? Okay, well, um.

Welcome to this, your guided meditation. It is just for you and not for anyone else on Cordite dot org dot au.

Find a comfortable place, somewhere you won't be disrupted. Like the floor next to my ringing phone, for instance, sure, fine. Okay, unclench your jaw.

Tsk tsk tsk tsk. Sk Sk Sk.

Like that, yes, now your eyebrows. Slacken your shoulders, feel the weight of your body on the lino. Move that relaxation downwards. Like that, like that. Now, inhale. Now, exhale.

Now, if you're like me and your head spins when you do these things, you might be asking:

> How do I stay alive boiling this fury far in me? When these listless, flaccid poems only salt right up my rage? Right? How could I use this bloody and limp tongue to dignify those I love? To offer more than symbols: empty and aware with no end?

We're all in that ugly, restless chorus shouting our shared fate.

Tk tk tk tk tsk, swoosh.

> *Hey yeah sorry, just step around them no they're fine it's okay — yeah she's just down the hall waiting for you. Did you bring your Medicare card? Okay, just leave it by the phone. No, I. Just hand it to me then, okay, third door. Remember to subscribe and hit the bell.*

If you're anything like me, you'll remind yourself — your every yawp of public pain is little more than a boreful background hum to others. The same is true for all among our midst — amidst all vaguely and horribly this.

We are choking on the smoke like our emphasytic parents, only catching little breaths atop our last. I certainly have no measure, that shameful uselessness we feel, except 164/94 and two new pills.

Shhhhh, tk tk tk tk, shhhhhhhh, hmmmmm

Notice without hard judgement, all the baking wrath in you. Every time it bubbles, bump into a new risk group.

Pick an affirmation to return to. There is no pressure. It only matters what it means to you. Anyway, each one is a humiliating gesture to our vast and weird oppression without end.

It is okay to surrender to that impulse. Let go of any tension.

Nothing you say will do anything but embarrass you. Also pretty much no doctor will prescribe benzos anymore. All of us will fail to scale with words the terror that we meet. If only there was something we could do when all around us buckles and dies other than, well, exposition.

Anyway, um, return to the breath. I have to make some calls.

The elastic on my tracksuit pants has given way.
I grab at it, loop an old hair tie around the bunch—
once, twice, thrice—
and make a material dickie (there's hair on the tie).
I bat it around as I wait for the kettle.

Outside pants will have a surge in sales, I had said
to a friend on Zoom.
And shoes, she said.
For a short moment, I get a little sad.
The kettle boils as I think about *Road House*

a Netflix watch from last Friday night.
I'd eaten a special brownie and it
had taken me some time to realise the film
was *actually* about the best bouncer in the business.
Sometimes, I can be a snob.

And I was probably fixating.
But can one be praised for being 'the best'
at something no one really cares about?
This was the first of my concerns. More important
was the fact that Dalton is *the worst* bouncer

I had ever seen. (I haven't seen a lot of bouncers).
I'm a cooler, Dalton says. As if that
is a cool thing to be. He cools things down,
doesn't resort to violence. This is his specialty.
This makes him the best in the business.

Pretty soon, the bar that hired him breaks out
in a brawl. Dalton steps in to cool things down, but
nothing cools. He must resort, quickly,
to his martial arts skills. There's a lot of violence.
The film features a lot more violence

and very little, if any, cooling. This left me
puzzled. I consoled myself with a bag
of spicy corn chips and a glass of milk.
And I'm pouring a bit of milk in a mug right
now. I pour it over granules of freeze-dried

Moccona. I'm an impatient person.
I like it when things are ready to go.
When that kettle clicks I like to pour and run.
Not run, exactly, but move relatively fast—
right now, as fast as my moccasins allow me to move,

back to my desk in the living room, adjacent
to the kitchen, my semi-permanent work situation.
I have two more meetings on Microsoft Teams
before knock-off, one of which is likely to get
heated. I wonder if I could be: best at filling in time

while the kettle boils; best at repurposing stretched
pants; best at staring down a heated conversation
on Microsoft Teams while my coffee cools beside me—
so good at the last, in fact, that others think I've frozen in time.
For some reason—inexplicable—I wonder:

Why would a villain be introduced into the world
of bouncing? I write poetry. The stakes are low and no one
cares. Say 'poet', you may as well say 'bouncer'. But things
in the poetry world can still get heated. I've seen
red faces, cold stares. Heard urban myths of punches thrown.

I could write the screenplay to a feature film called
Poet House. A poet laureate comes in to a literary community
to cool the jets of rival factions. The poet is paid
so handsomely, in fact, that the community hub defaults
on their rent, and collapses completely. Best all-round fantasy.

A poet never cooled a fight. 'Best poet' is like
'best bouncer'. The trophy is a little
joke. Through the window, I can see the sun
has emerged from behind clouds. I get a little sad.
(Weather exerts this pressure). I realise that

all this thinking has cooled my coffee. And that,
when this is over, I'll have to shuck my moccasins,
strap myself into a bra. I'll have to shelve my busted
tracksuit pants, my material dickie, which made me feel
so much more stress free, so nonchalant. So cool.

Her Late Hand | JAYA SAVIGE

Like some deathtrap whose   wiring hadn't
been earthed, the live house of her   handwriting
remains unsafe. Here is mosquito   din, gnat whir
and midge language, transcribed   and writhing;
and there is where her   hard tin wing
nicked a smidgen from the moon's   thawing rind.

Look, a whisper, *here is the*   *nth drawing I*
made of a wounded   *hart, winding …*

There must be better ways to   draw night in
but this is mine: take a holograph and   wring it, hand
over hand,   twining hard,
then drape it, still damp, over the   thin wan grid
of an insect zapper. Maybe it's a   Darwin thing
and extinction's but a glut of   inward night,
a crow with comic timing in a   ward, hinting
that only those with the   right DNA win.

Reserve your bitter myr-   rh, giant wind.
Give us one last nocturne on the baby   grand within
her heaving   writing hand.

How to Love Like a Horse | SHASTRA DEO

after Mindy Gill's 'A Kind of Paradise'

What I know about desire is horses
who aren't hungry can't be owned
by anyone. The horse, she bows to no-one
—well, she bows
only for bribe, wheedle and charm, only
for a patch of fresh clover, or an apple to chomp
to pieces. A horse is a good thing to think on
when I can't speak neatly. Our jaws
working in tandem. And maybe she bows
to carry you from there to where
-ever the earth allows us to walk
to my fetlocks, knowing
that to love is to sometimes keep
one's feet off the ground,
and to look on a horizon is to see only
the past. A horse is a good place to be,
strategically. And here I am understanding
that horses know to wait
for their happiness: the swing of a muzzle
into the chest of her beloved, a hand muscling in
at the withers. That big horse heart at rest.
Eating the clover at dusk, knowing
the next day will be twice
as lucky.

the day after the 'inadequate' club opened its doors they were ripped off their hinges.

~~

shoes so casual you couldn't wear them   but their footprints left nothing to the imagination.

~~

the avocado sandal served its purpose, the lettuce spinner jealous as a chilli.

~~

we're at home so often
we actually live here

~~

the difference between a corn
thin and a corn thick
is the difference between
a mouth and a small toe

~~

when the wildcard
becomes the greeting
card there's not
much to say

~~

you misread 'she remembered her wet rainbow'—should have been
'rainshoes'—accidental therapy, or embarrassment

~~

lore abiding [or make yer own grammar]

after the damper
is cooked in the bush
oven 'just slice her up'

~~

breezeblock

a trim grammar of green lawns
sprawl of pine needles across
the syntax of pools   mow town
confers in the courtyards
parsing the time of day

~~

umbillical cord:
you pay for it

~~

fleur de lies

in the far left column
of the deaths and funeral
notices page—
        BOULDERS WANTED
Boulders greater than 1500mm
required in Arcadia (free tip)

~~

siesta

grime of discarded scribble
failed poems like worn
out money in some dust
riddled bazaar   a donkey
brays into your diary of
fleas

~~

active wear
death stare
let's do a runner

~~

i am working when
i'm not working and
not working when i'm
working   i work while
i sleep and i sleep
while i work this
is a life worth living

~~

small world

i've been thinking
of those images of the
ceauseşcus after
their executions—did
they know the assads
were they friends roll
on (non) elective
affinities

~~

world news

humanitarian windows or
brave restaurants

~~

sydney -

you will probably find
the collected works of
emily dickinson in
the fiction section—

~~

lustgarten

ben and dotty day
got their measle shots
too late

~~

porkie

waiting on a bench for a pad
thai takeaway i bone up on
the free gossie glossies   gosh—
a miracle diet: just spray windex
on that plate of food, rain hail or
shine

~~

rind

overheard at a francis bacon exhibition

he's not much of a bird
drawer   he should stick
to people

~~

[transport]

wearing retro german
intellectual spectacles
reading danielle steel

~~

[jam fancy]

he slipped in the corridors
of power   he was honoured
in the hall of fame

~~

[popping up]

an art book 'sigmar polke: we petty
bourgeois!' has been catalogued as 'we
pretty bourgeois'

Hyphenated | THUY ON

Cognitive dissonance is an Asian woman
who has to carry her grandmother's special phở
in her lukewarm blood to impress at dinner parties,
be after-schooled in strings and numbers:
a hothouse orchid with no outside breeze

she has to be an ingenue unwise to the ways of men
who largely want her for her smallness
the wriggling cheongsam the flutter fingers
then stillness: bamboo waist and water lily serene
lickable caramel against their burly chests

everyone loves a happy migrant story:
leaky prawn trawler to valedictorian
a seam of jade trapped in ancestral dust
to be extracted and rubbed to sheen
she has to blaze a trail to prove she's keen.

i am writing in vignettes because all we have are fragments
| LUJAYN HOURANI

it rains on eid al fitr
my family spends four hours
in my living room without
the heater on we do not talk
we scroll and read
and listen and scroll and sit
and scroll and post
and watch my phone dies
before dinner

it is always about footage

my friend DMs me
have u seen that video of Toni Morrison
where she talks about how
no matter how bad things got
she always knew
that she was morally superior
to the racists in the world

in 2006 Mr Hyrnczak organised a fundraiser
for Gaza i was in year eight
and proud and smug and excited
that for a few days things were about us

i am writing in vignettes because
all we have are fragments

on monday
israeli forces fire on
Palestinians at al Aqsa

on tuesday
i stay home from work

on wednesday we wake up to
israel bombs Gaza

on thursday
i see a video of israeli cops and lynch mobs
breaking into a house in haifa
the owners ramming back the door
if a screech had a body
it would vibrate like that
the camera is shaking
someone has retweeted it
with *this is nakba*
this is what happened
to my family in 1948
now we have footage

i am writing in vignettes
because it is always about footage

i do not know when
this poem will be published
but by then these words
will have fossilised

i do not remember my dreams last night
just fragments
that return in whips a ponytail
a clothes hanger my dad
red plaid shirt
the tail of a prawn
chewing and swallowing

i read *fascists among us*
on the tram to the protest
to remind myself:
racists do have morals
they're just not good ones

last year we went viral
normalisation and in
2019
annexation and in
2018
the march of return

it does not matter
when this poem is published
these fragments always fossilise
only to get dug up a year later

it storms the night before the protest
and the latch
on my bedroom window
has not been repaired
i lie on my back and think of the rain
and wind and hail teaming up to explode
the brittle seams of plastic

[Who paid for your passage?]
    The blood that burned the brightest
    was always the one we followed.

[Is there a clock in your father's bedroom?]
    When he slept, silver wheat grew
    from the sweat of his clothes.

    The morning always found
    a quiet place to kneel.

[Is someone forcing you to come here?]
    I don't understand the question.

[Who were your neighbours?]
    The name *Yu Yan*. The name *Ying Yue*.
    The word *yùn dòng*. The clouds—sliding
    like *Wang Shu's* wet slippers across the hallway.
    The field—the field inside the finger.
    The golden doorknobs wrapped in a blanket.
    The loose joints rattling the ginger-jar.
    The salt in the curve of a pinnae.
    The sound *womb* glistening the air.
    The strand of hair lengthening in the spine of a book.
    The ocean forgetting our names.
    The sky thirsting for our bodies.
    Our bodies thirsting for the sky.
    The country—her country—welling in the afterglow.

[Who paid for your passage?]
    Unable to speak,
    the dark thawed around us.

    We held birds like candles.

    A child mistook the snow
    for his mother.

[*What direction does the front of your house face?*]
   When we were lost,
   I pulled the curve of moonlight
   from the wet of his lips
   into a sickle between my palms.

   It always spun South.

[*What pieces of furniture were in your living room?*]
   The radio—the father inside the radio.
   The box of chalk. The pocket mirror.
   The teeth—the jade inside the teeth.
   The map that shrivels in the moonlight.
   The wax that blooms in the bone.
   The chopsticks—slid—into the holes of coins.
   The shadows braided on the clothesline.
   The window that breaks like an eardrum.
   The wind drawing names in the ashtray.
   The bayberry bleeding on the tongue.
   The body—thrashing—like a blanket in the mouth.
   The candied ginger—goldening on the table.
   The breasts—her breasts—swelling ripe in the heat.

[*What is your final destination?*]
   Could you please repeat the question?

[*What is your final destination?*]
   Where the shadow pauses
   at the edge of a meadow
   into the shape of a deer.

[*What is your name?*]

[*What is your name?*]

The Important Things | AUDREY MOLLOY

i.m. Marianne Ihlen

There's a word in Scots Gaelic—sgrìob—
which refers to the tingle on the upper lip
just before you take a sip of whisky.
We are talking—after the burial,
now they've allowed funerals again—
across a table no bigger than a dinner plate
about those we've lost to the virus,
and whisky or whiskey—the important things—
when Roy Buchanan comes on the jukebox
and I can almost taste the light
film of sweat on your skin.
I should have known it right then:
an inventor will always be curious,
and that here, in this bar, months from now,
you will sit in false darkness
with another muse,
while on our white-board veranda,
its double swing written by Harper Lee,
I'll dip my best bristle brush
in tin after tin of green—
viridian, sap, olive, emerald—
and slap paint mixed with salt onto timber shades
until every trace of off-white is erased.
I'll forgive you, in time, everything
but the way you changed my name
in the song that made you famous,
trimming a syllable to rhyme with *began*;
the irony of that, since it was the end,
and not even our story,
though all unhappy stories resemble each other.
But let's not catastrophize,
we haven't yet begun, and right here, right now,
in The Fiddler's Arms,
there's a feeling coming over me,
a surface tension close to my upper lip,
that no English word can describe.

In Abbotsford: 4pm | ELENA GOMEZ

I'm a dip in The Suburb, I go straight down
across eight lanes of traffic, I'm picking up
speed, below the underpass, If I stop it's for
another, nobody even looks, I've been told
I'm responsible. It's grim, it's past the oval
that was for footy but now for dogs off their leads,
it's like this, I'm back, here again I can believe it,
I'm plugged, in to conspiracy theories, celebrity gossip,
in my head, I'm a gazelle, there's not one limit
to the self-delusion, weeded for this undertaking,
there's a moment, at the descent that takes a breath,
but you still need to watch out for some cars, they
backed out, they think of the lovely house in
New Hampshire, I wonder if I'll live in a lovely house,
but not that kind of lovely house, I'm also friends
with people in lovely and other kinds of houses, are we
measuring incorrectly, small cloth stain is a lie,
it's a nesting arc for brides, a bromide, is the other
word, is a word, the ground for 3 metres is caked in it,
my long-dead dog loves it, where is the tab left for this,
where is the tab left behind, I am turned on when scolded
for having too many tabs left open, it's not a huge upward
drip in the garden, I never looked close enough at
what grows there, it's often the part to take over women,
pushing prams and family bike rides, it's probably the
slow rise, I was making the same red lentil coconut curry,
for a while I was ready to try something new, but when
did that make anyone feel any better, it's a point of maybe
1.5km before the house paddock arrives, I'm too nostalgic
about things, I'm told, like when I look up old family
homes on real estate dot com, I fear that one day I will
decide I can live in an outer suburb, I consider friends
a bonus, my rehab is working (I like the exercise in the
position Right Lateral Recumbent), I can feel it in the hip
flexors, and surrounds, the hip flexors are destroyed
in modern bodies, I was deterred to them, my body is with
the rest of the purpose, do other poets obsess with

excellence or are they just able to be in the world, I enjoy
the large black pigs but their pens are lately empty, one
of them is named Mabel or Maple, the sheep are usually
pretty boring, I was reading Leopardi some mornings ago,
the recluse, is it significant, is it significant I read him in the
morning, the pages are thinner than a bible's, what is it he
says about poetry's function as delight?: 'the great majority
of useful works bring pleasure indirectly, showing how we can
obtain it. Poetry brings it immediately, provides it for us'
and also: 'usefulness is not the purpose of poetry although
poetry is useful' and 'to give delight is the natural office
of poetry', earlier I had left a note here commanding me
to find the quote, there are goats in a mound today minus
four months, they rest their heads on each other's backs,
I consider space and personal space and needs,
I am inclined to the community, I am not a people person,
I am in the community but from afar, I am mediated
in some of these ways I won't list right now, one afternoon
it finishes raining, there is a large cow being eyed
by a toddler, I am on a science fiction bend, I used to get
fatigue in my thighs, I used to be weaker in my limbs,
I prefer to put in effort, and if not I enjoy being a slug,
which is preferred over a snail, I hope I do not need to
explain this, but if I must, you could guess how I do it,
we're spreading new facts on weightbearing in lobbies,
this next part is important: blobfish in its natural habitat,
I saw photos of the blobfish like this, it is structurally intact,
the blobfish is not mopey-faced or jelly dollop in its
unaltered state, it is fish-like, its blob shape appears in
the course of its removal, it is destroyed by the new levels,
by the atmosphere, by lesser pressures, I'm back down
the river. There is a woman throwing a ball into the water
and her large hound (which is what I call dogs to sound
Romantic) jumps in to play 'aquafetch', to retrieve the ball
he has swum to the middle, I wonder if the woman
must be attentive to the speed of the river and needs to make
a calculation either of her throw reach or her dog's ability,

though it's a big dog, I am swept easily by currents
so I am sensitive to this problem, you never step into
the river, I'll make a new curry but it's sort of an old one,
I did this for a while with a different type of chickpea,
my mother told me about them and they're small and brown
and nutty not like the big white garbanzo beans, I often go
on the hunt for them when the whim arises, I do not often
remember to do this with intention, this is true
for most cuisines or ingredients, I decide to incorporate
it, a menu for the house, I get to the bottom of the staircase,
I run up, at the top I feel triumphant, my body survives
but is unhappy with me, it acts betrayed, when I put it
through a straining run it is compact, my body does not
accept apologies, it complies with sleep
in my loud thoughts. We are happy in the fog.

In My Fortieth Year, I Realise I Am Not Them | EILEEN CHONG

The moon rises above clouds.
In the cold light, all is grey, and white.

Night sky turns on a paper wheel.
Stars are silvered, immutable.

The only sound: a deer scarer
filling, emptying, and filling again.

We were travelling over the ice in summer. In the city the light was blinding: it gave you headaches just looking out the window, even at night with shades on. Bobby was in town. He called up asking for loose change and also to say hello, and somehow we made a plan to skip out. The summer was just winding up: I rang my boss at the Magic Wand Carwash and said I had tonsillitis, and we caught the ferry at four in the afternoon. The boat was full of college kids being rowdy; Bobby and me shared a packet of Reese's Puffs and stared out at the ice and blue ridges of mountains floating by. If you didn't count the first day, which was only an evening really, it was all up exactly two weeks we spent together, in various hotels and motels across the border. The best place was the Holiday Inn at Whitehorse, where the sheets had crisp edges and the maids left little heart-shaped candies on the pillows. Bobby had some sharks on his tail, so we called ourselves Mr. and Mrs. Smith and paid in cash. Eventually we stopped worrying and had a fine time. In the Yukon the air was clean, you could breathe great lungfuls and feel free. Then late one night Bobby got a call from an old friend who said Thelma was asking after him in the usual places, and that he'd better show up somewhere soon or else. Our money had about run out, so we hitched down the Klondike, sometimes in big trucks, sometimes in dinky RVs, and once with a whole busload of nuns on their way to pay a visit to Saint Thérèse. They sang hymns and played Rummy while we sat in the front and watched the sun rise like a red eye over the ice. When we got back he split, the troubles began. I knew it would be the same as before, but there was no use feeling sorry about it. Juneau can be like that.

Lament for Fieldmice | DAVID BROOKS

I believe in no deity
and the religion I was born into
is dangerous and hollow as a drum,
but I won't accept that these great trees I stand among
are not the volutes and capitals
of a vast, inconsecrate cathedral, or that Henry
the used-to-be ram is not high priest,
the ducks and cockatoos and currawong
apostles and prophets of a different sky,
the rats and fieldmice the local
council's just poisoned—who'd bring
me whispers as they passed—
mystics and hapless seraphim
now twisting in agony in the summer grass.

Letter to a Dead Parent | DAVID MUSGRAVE

Whenever I look at your grandson,
I see dad's face, but you're the one
or several parts of one, who animates his rage
and cheek, just as how the other day
at two-and-a-quarter, he put a soccer ball
into a bucket and called it 'ice cream', licking it.
It's as if you're still alive, but blind to survival,
counting 'one, two, five, eighteen, twenty four'
with the precision of a train timetable,
opened at random. How you would have loved
to see him, even in your last unravelling,
the way he pushes away my hand
if I try to turn the page too soon, or how
he will stare blankly ahead, deaf to anything
I say before slyly looking sideways at me,
then laughing. This week I've drawn
fifty seven big fish and three hundred
and forty two little fish and thirty eight
spouting whales. It's hard to believe
that part of me could go on being, let alone
this tenacious chain that links to you, here,
where a breeze bends the corridor
around its cold and touches your hair.
A lot has happened since you've gone:
this pandemic; it's strange how there
are no individuals, just a society where
you can hide but can't run.
Your grandson brings me a horse's head
in the palm of his hand, separated from its body
by an accident, and overcome by penitence,
says 'sorry daddy' over and over, lying face down
on the ground. I didn't teach him this,
so where did he learn it? I'm sorry that you never got to see
his frown, breathing over a shark or Boss Boonga
in the Big House at the end of the road.
But when he points at agave plants
along the side path, tells me 'dinosaur'

I dine on sores, or dining saws remind me
of the older truths, the hardening of bone
or its mirror, sagging skin, a voice that's broken
into words, or words flowering into the wave
of a hand, 'goodbye outside, goodbye diningsaur'.

It's simple: you either believe another world is possible or you don't.
To believe is to be on the side of rock-throwers, to find a rock to throw.
Recto: the story of the world contains a chapter for each innovation
that found and ruined yet unimagined zones of rest, pleasure, flesh,
and study; a chapter for each gadget that extended the zone of work to
non-work; a chapter for each technique of watching, holding, frisking,
patting, searching, emptying, surveilling, surveying, weighing,
shaking. What is it to write a poem about love or to sound a note that
gets lost in the chorus or to move to the wrong rhythm which is, of
course, the real rhythm? Proudhon once said that 'All property is theft'.
The containment of what was stolen is the violence of state, which is
another way of describing settlement, which is another way of naming
a murderous pathology, which is another way to identify a condition
that can never be satisfied. But what if that which is made into property
cannot be contained? Moten and Harney say: 'All property is loss
because all property is the loss of sharing'. Fuck your property, we
say in chorus with those who set fire to the servants and protectors of
the commodity form. And yet, as we learn from the burnin and the
lootin, property cannot be contained. 'We survive only insofar as all
property remains vulnerable to sharing', preach Moten and Harney. In
our pockets: a handful of stars. In our pockets: miscellaneous crumbs,
half-chewed trinkets, scraps of a meal we have eaten before. To share
ourselves is to remain on the run, to desire our own loss so that we
might find each other. Love is the condition of our assembly, which
is another way to say that we consent not to be a single being, which
is another way to say that we survive only by being together, which is
another way to describe friendship, which is another way to begin the
arduous task of abolishing the settler state, which is another way to
invoke communism. We have nothing but love for the children of the
stones. When we dance to El-Funoun, we move against the cop and the
soldier, the border and the state. A shared exhaustion, against the toxic
solidarity of statecraft. Verso: the story of the world contains a chapter
for each invention that found yet unimagined tools for struggle, that
found a way to reclaim pleasure, flesh, and study from every hellish
nook of the workplace; a chapter for each gadget that extended the fight
for non-work in the extensive and receding fringe of work; a chapter
for each technique of grifting, shaving, chipping, siphoning, cribbing,

poaching, and pocketing. History's front and back page dialectic allows for a different reading strategy. Against the grim arc from left to right we read the encoded dictionary of survival and conviviality, a recipe in reverse for how to turn the skims of tobacco, skins of milk, rings of a barrel, rims of a ship, slips of silk or steel shavings into a meal, a dress, a home, a kitchen table, a study book, a parade, a song, a child. The shape of things to come can only be known from inside. Unionised port workers blocked the shipment of arms from Italy to Israel. 'We will not be an accomplice in the massacre of the Palestinian people', the workers' statement read as they held the ship in its dock. The story of struggle is always shared. One stone against invasion, another against enclosure, another against possession. We write a love poem as an act of solidarity.

The Vibrant Committee is measuring levels.
The Standard Committee keeps issuing gestures.
The Works Committee is careful in print.
The Comms Committee is mindful of content.
The Committee of Nice is pure radiance,
unlike the Committee of Pure Radiance.
The Investment Committee is trimming horizons.
The Planning Committee is along for the ride.
Afloat on a raft of measures and ideals,
the Budget Committee was on your side.
The Adjustments Committee is upskilling.
The Impact Committee is finetuning.
The Corrections Committee is subcontracting.
The Benefits Committee is downsizing.
The Vision Committee has footballers on it,
as does the Committee for Public Art.
What you mistook for a blossoming garden
is really the Committee for an unknown reform.
The Committee of Trust is mending fences.
The Committee of Crisis will last through the rules.
The Intentions Committee is nude as ivory.
The Committee of Youth has just realised.
The Committee for Unscripted Tears
is dissolving.

The Map of Home | MONA ZAHRA ATTAMIMI

Emptying my mother's home, a map—
the colour of tea stains, marked by rivers
                and oceans, a compass rose,
wind symbols over Asia, and trees and roots

                belonging to women who'd sewn date-pips
on to their black tunics and left palm
                leaves to dry between holy books—I found,
among seventy bottles

                of human hair. A bottle each for a year
of her life—that was how my mother's mind
                ticked. I stooped over them,
touched the jars with my ankles. The glass

                was cold. Next to the map was a wooden chest.
The weight of her death caused me
                to lean forward and trip
over a shoe. I hit the chest with my elbows

                and what was revealed were pages
of her diary, patched and quilted into
                a long funeral shroud. Her writings
were prolific, dating back to 1953. She wrote

                on the day her father died and when
her mother gave her away to a lady who'd
                lost her voice on the ship to the Moluccas; she wrote
of the time she was trapped inside

                old rooms, and when she travelled in the tunnels
of a colonised city; she wrote of the time
                she gave birth and died as a woman; and she
wrote of the time when her memories nearly

killed her, of how having a daughter chained
her to the table where she drew the map
of a country snaked in rivers and stained
in tea. Her funeral shroud was elaborately

designed in the shape of her will. The outline,
in avocado green, declared that the house,
after she was gone, had to be burnt,
the jars of hair to float on the rivers,

and the girl-child, who'd found her shroud
and ate the words, must inherit the map.
Her spell has stayed on my sleeves, it roams
the sea and the stony cliffs they call

the Matriarch. Whenever I pass
the ashes of winter homes and hear crying
in the dry wind, she whispers: *have you
buried my shroud, have you kept my will in the urn?*

つ ✿ₒ_ₒ✿つ (＿×＿)

the BWS is now a BWyaasssssS as in yass queen as in yasssss gay pride as in yass we co-opted this lingo from black queer communities on the other side of the world as in BeerWineSpirits is now a place to drink down some black queer liberation on land stolen that locks up blak queer bodies if maybe they've had a bit too much BeerWineSpirits but won't lock up the others who snarl as you walk down the street hand in hand with ya misso on ya way to have a drink

(ɔ◉ᵕ◉)ɔ ♥ ≧◉ᵕ◉≦

GayTMs it's like an ATM but it's gayer holds your hand after but doesn't leave a number or maybe moves in on tuesday or maybe pays for medication yours or nan's or someone else's or helps get some kid a mental health care plan to figure out why their body don't seem right but won't grant rights and won't write a cheque and won't write to government about bodies that don't fit between two tick-boxes but will give you the option for a receipt thank you see you next time don't forget your card don't forget your cash don't forget your yasssss queen

≧★ᵕ★≦ (/◕ヮ◕)/*:·°✧

and the google map shows the route in rainbow to the stadium where exec gays and clever rich straights can have front row seats behind the gate to the genuine gays and all those genuine straights who thought it was be so cute to be on the corporate float this year and march alongside the police who would absolutely never systematically target the queer community and who are absolutely not built on a legacy of doing just that and who absolutely don't uphold a colony that enforces an ideology that makes no space for non-normative bodies just ask the next lot oh yay it's the liberal party what a special day what a lovely float thanks for spending all that money so everyone could have a vote (ɔ˘ ³(ˆ◡ˆc)   ]:->   :^)

instagram is for mardi gras and google is for mardi gras and absolut is for mardi gras and vodafone is for mardi gras and sydney is for mardi gras a tourism campaign and mardi gras is for profits under a rainbow banner that holds no one up but gives enough rope to make sure that there is one version of a rainbow and it fits the gaze of execs who had to work hard to be so correct and even went to their cousin's wedding two grooms and look this is what the community want and look this is a community with cash and look money is for mardi gras and mardi gras was a protest but protest isn't sexy when it's hard or anti-excess so you can wrap up your bigotry in glitter and call it progress for a weekend and none of these corporations speak up when they come for our rights but hashtag loveislove when everything is over won and done

(/◕ヮ◕)/ (^o^) (✿◠‿◠)

the blaks get down on a knee and it doesn't make the broadcast and the cops get run out run onto and it doesn't make the broadcast and the community floats get their thirty seconds and the corporate floats get their seventy seconds and the protest before the march is the family event that gets run out run onto by those cops who tried to block queer loving protest and on the walk home down oxford street dreaming we get heckled and listen to others screaming and men with iphones ask us to kiss for their private archive and strangers with long range lenses take photos for who knows what archive not asking yass queen mardi gras dreaming sydney wears its corruptness never fearing and no need to shame your rum colony feeding rum colony breeding more cops who can run out run onto those who can't afford to pay thank you thank you sydney for our special diluted day

(◡.◡) (_!_) (^◡^)

Metal bird | THERESA PENANGKE ALICE

Awaye!
Arrware yanhele alkere
Atarkentyeme, ahelhe altywere ilemele
Thipe akngerre
Apenhele
Nelheke
Arrenityeke

Listen! That loud sound
It cracks my stomach too
As it pierces the sky open
The land and the plains open
The wind scoops it into the air
And puts it down on land like a bird
The land shakes and prepares
For the metal bird to land safely

Translated from Arrernte by Theresa Penangke Alice

Micröbius Tract(ion)

I.
i,
softly
machine

love to
swallow
the water
w e t t i n g
my throat
fielding
viral   im/-
probabilities

i, vibrancy
ma~~~chine
—honey bees taking
me for a flower—

like to
swish the
water btwn
my teeth first
feeling   the
fear of contagion
now dressed in
the membranes of
big girl hydration

i,   *ma*   *chine*   (backbone of an animal or
                                                              mountain ridge)

we,   ~~~   *sheen*   (shine or cause to shine
                                                              softly)

when
in travelling through
extra- invertebrate
infrastructures
ram up   against
dam(n)ed walls to
flounce, ruche
& gather
honing
the pleats

i, mine   *sheen*   [swelling
ganglia
am told to   copper
swallow   fibre
the water   optic
nerve]

i, hesitate
to swallow
the water
then pause
to   ask:
what
is caulked with
fluoride here?
what
cloakings of
microbes, flora, cilia
what
likes &   loves
what
extractive
regimes
steal my
water?

what   conditions
here   inebriate
my   water? I
mean   how
exactly   is
it   drunk?

i, of
machination

    analgesic
      fogging of
        a   route
       from where
        the brachia
           e   x   t   e   n   d   s
      away from
      the body bac-
     terial flowering
  all   over it

i, am of *this*
machine

one condition nested
  inside the other like
    angiosperm
    is both   fruit
   seeding flower
  the containing of
  an order of ovum
  that is also   ore

    it is a heady
     hooch of
     a task
       this
       machine

II.

in   the early
stages   of
development   a loss of
b u c c o p h a r y n g e a l
m e m b r a n e
opens   the
tract   to
amniotic   fluid   —a mix of
water   and
electrolytes
and   later
in   the sugar, scraps of
later   stages vagrant DNA,
of   development fats, proteins,
a   loss   of piss, and shit.[1]
p r o p r i e t a r y
m e m b r a n e
opens   the
self   to
world   to
fluid   :   a
s u b s t a n c e
that   has
no   fixed
shape   and
yields   easily
to   external
p r e s s u r e

—*we do not breathe.*
nor do we drown. [2]

III.
too much
nitrogen and
not   enough
oxygen creates
Deadly   Blooms
in the   water.
how should we
drink   your
neuro-toxi-
cant capital
seventh skin
of sin that this bac-
terium of care—like a
committed   handling of
orange-scented
antidepresant—
palpate

i, wish to
acknowledge
that our imported
skins are teeming
differently with the
same in-
visible aerobes
and bacilli—
the requiring of
oxygen &
the
pro-
duction
of dis-
ease—that
our ancestors
practice
in these
fields

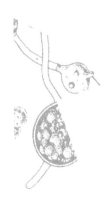

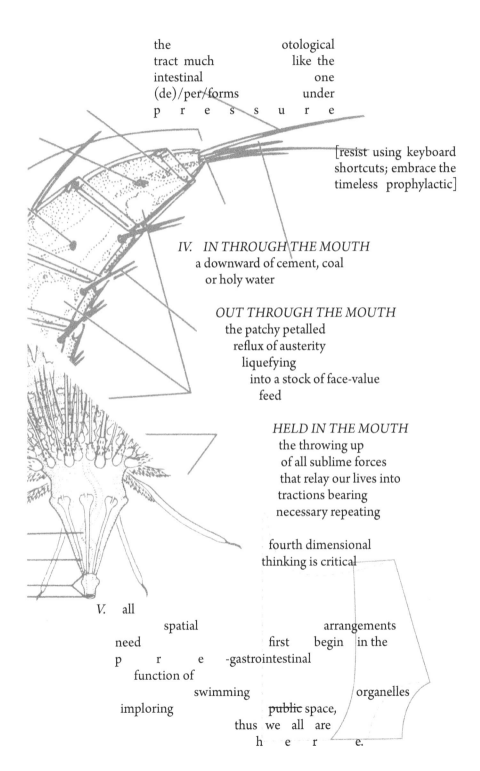

the   otological
tract much   like the
intestinal   one
(de)/per/forms   under
p   r   e   s   s   u   r   e

[resist using keyboard
shortcuts; embrace the
timeless prophylactic]

IV. *IN THROUGH THE MOUTH*
a downward of cement, coal
or holy water

OUT THROUGH THE MOUTH
the patchy petalled
reflux of austerity
liquefying
into a stock of face-value
feed

HELD IN THE MOUTH
the throwing up
of all sublime forces
that relay our lives into
tractions bearing
necessary repeating

fourth dimensional
thinking is critical

V. all
spatial   arrangements
need   first   begin in the
p   r   e   -gastrointestinal
function of
swimming   organelles
imploring   public space,
thus we all are
h   e   r   e.

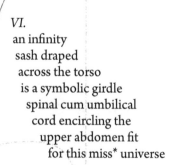

VI.
an infinity
sash draped
across the torso
is a symbolic girdle
spinal cum umbilical
cord encircling the
upper abdomen fit
for this miss* universe

a fixed   sash draped
b   e   t   w   e   e   n
two vertical   bollards
encircling the   steel rim
of a   water   fountain
powered   cold   by coal
          power   is   a
b   a   r   r   i   e   r
to   basic   universal
rights to   clean water —being in public
                           w i t h o u t
                           c o n s u m i n g
                           is   the   biggest
                           threat to those
                           in control   .3

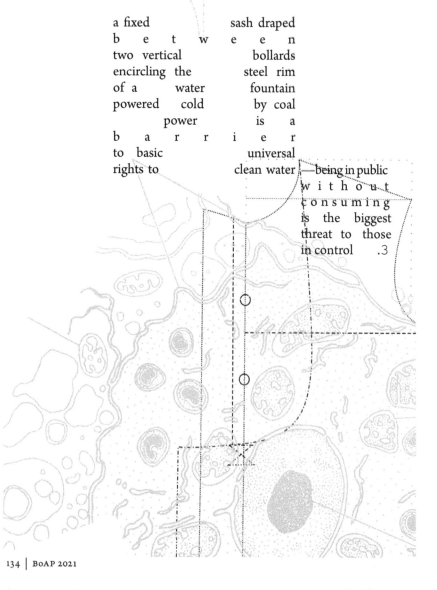

VII.

shield shrimp
survive hidden
y e a r s
between rains

we   walk
a r o u n d
b r e a t h i n g
un   easy
through   our
gill   feet

re   member
to   unpick
your   weft
prior   to
a d o r n i n g
your   tongue

r e d r e s s
the   fabric
lead beating
soils guttered
beds   our
t u m e s c e n t
b o d i e s
sleep under

add
water
to three
hundred
more year
old sea-
weed
bind
consoli-
date
your
gums

lay
down
your
alibis
and
pro-
ceed
with
a
vo-
tive

1. Sophie Lewis, *Full Surrogacy Now: Feminism Against Family*, Verso, London & New York, 2019, p. 160.
2. ibid.
3. @dividedpublishingltd instagram post, 10 March, 2021.

MIRABILIA | LISA GORTON

> *if that which is at all were not forever*
> —Marianne Moore, 'The Pangolin'

It is its
own order—scaled mammal that can
      spiral itself in
armour safe in the lion's jaws—
      it is toothless, its
      belly is naked,
its only predator is man—
      Adept alike of
dry savannah and equatorial canopies
it walks on riverbeds—Huyghen van Linschoten, a
      Dutchman in Goa,
when fishers hauled one out, thought it
a strange fish—
it being middle-sized-dog sized,
      elephant-footed,
snorting like a hog—
its head tail legs all cased in scales
      harder than iron
or steel—
      Mild moving anvil,
they hewed at it with weapons—and
it rolled up
and could not be prised open—Its
picture, for a wonder, they sent to the King of Spain—
In the pouch of its eyelid its
near-blind round black eye has written
underneath—
I
have seen it—
It goes by smell, its
      way of going—through
the vast plain-like stretches or dank
leafmould straight up trees—

could solve the problem
of depicting a mind thinking so that the idea
is not separate from the act
      of experiencing it—
imagined mind that goes subtly
      reasoning forwards
on an unforseen line surely
to the place—
When it
      comes to it, it goes
nose shut ears shut eyes shut headfirst
      into what it likes—
it bathes in ants, it
      is particular—
      wries its tongue (free-drawn
line out
from its snout's blunted pencil tip)
      against a wrong taste—
It goes on hind legs—its finger-
      length-clawed hands it folds
one over another or at
      times taps down—it can
carve concrete—
Its tail its counterweight it holds
      with hoopskirt-like up-
rightness
      (yearly with raw silk
pink pinking-shear-trimmed
      pangopup bustle)
under which its legs go with a
      separate light ease
unexpected under armour—
its armour is not put on—the
      snake's head helmet be-
tween its eyes at its nape outspreads
in overlapping scallop-shell-ridged scales of ochre,
      amber, olive-brown

each edged with lighter bands
       so when it goes—with
wave-through-wave
movement along a branch or in
       night grasslands as one
unbroken wave—its repeating
       varied scales track light
like a principle of growth—each
       one replacing each
other's vanishing—as if that which is could be for-
                   ever—
       It is toothless, its
       belly is naked—
its only predator is man—

Some phrases are taken from Jan Huyghen van Linschoten's travel writing, Randall Jarrell's review of Elizabeth Bishop ('written underneath, "I have seen it"'), and Marianne Moore's letter to Ezra Pound ('could solve the problem of depicting a mind thinking so that the idea is not separate from the act of experiencing it').

1. Black

Uncle takes us walking on Yuin Country.
He shows us overgrown bush grapevine wrestling
with sarsaparilla and gums.
He tells us blackfullas would have burnt this back long ago
if they were allowed.
He makes us tea in a billy, gets told by a ranger to put it out.
Fire ban. A month later Uncle loses everything
returns home to find a half-burnt roo stumbling around.

2. Indigo

My sister and I drive from Cadigal to Naarm.
Smoke shepherds us down passed the bulrushes of Wodonga.
We breathe blue sky for the first time in months.

3. Brown

Out where Wiradjuri and Wailwan meet
marsh dries to desert. 3,000 hectares of reed beds burn.
It doesn't make the six pm news.

4. Orange

A friend and I swing in hammocks up in Gringai bush.
All the grass is dead. They are feeding the pademelons
sweet potato.

5. Silver

My cousin and I go camping at New Years'.
We meet where saltwater and freshwater wed
on Worimi Country. We bunker down in tents as sirens pass
lightning wreaks havoc on drought washed hills.
We prepare to evacuate.

6. Yellow

I travel with my sister to visit Mob
on Biripi and Dungutti Country.
We eat chip sandwiches like we did as kids
with Dad in the shadows of Wollumbin.
We watch Nan eat lemons
from the tree we sit under
while smoke from grass fires linger.

7. Purple

After the Jacaranda blooms, we go into lock down.
We are locked in together on Gadigal land.
I work from my bedroom and feel more trapped than ever.
A manager tells me she heard an Aboriginal woman
on Sky News say blak breathlessness isn't a problem.
Not in Australia.
I can't argue. I need to pay bills.

8. Violet

Rio Tinto rapes Juukan Gorge.
Rio Tinto makes final dividend payment totalling $3.6 billion.
Rio Tinto's share price returns to six-month high.

9. Gold

Someone complains about doing all of Brighton
the vulnerable are Rapunzeled in towers.
Essential workers are scared of hunger
too scared to tell managers
they live with a positive case.

10. Red

USyd calls cops on student protest of less than twenty.
USyd's Vice Chancellor increases number
of students in tutorials to thirty.
Hundreds of students return to protest at USyd

11. White

I travel with my cousin to Seal Rocks,
we camp by melting white Worimi shores.
All the seals are lost.
We try to have a discussion about protecting
cultural knowledge. We are interrupted by a neoliberal
tells us there is no point, someone will steal it for profit.
He leaves before we can reply.
He shows off his drone to private school friends.
He doesn't realise he stands in a midden.

12. Green

I walk with my mother through curated rainforest
on Gumbaynggirr land.
It feels like the first weekend
in history. It is the first we are allowed to travel.
I walk with my father on Gumbaynggirr coast.
The winter sun, cool sand and breeze are medicine.
Country mothers me and I feel replenished.
Towards the end of winter
the drought is breaking
on the six pm news.

Mother on Men | PETRA WHITE

Mother what is a man?
Put on your red hat,
but don't let a man see you wearing red.
Mother what is a man?
A man is a piece of burnt toast, a glass of vinegar.
Never pour a man into your eye, never eat one at night.
Mother what is a man?
The white stew of cabbage moths
simmering around my cup of tea.
Mother what is a man?
It is the shadow of an eagle over the man-mouse
that makes him tremble like a living thing.
Mother what is a man?
Things, electric ruffles, places to hide,
he is vast and gargantuan, a piece of rubber.
Mother what is a man?
I found him in the rubbish, I loved him back to health,
he perched on my finger like a friendly sparrow.
I was waiting for him to bite me,
I waited a long time. Didn't I tell you this?
When he grew strong I ate dust and capers.
Mother what is a man?
He walks upright like a toad,
I mean, like a cloud.
Mother what is a man?
Never look him in the eye, bow your head,
walk backwards away from him.
If he comes to you with love
burn all the teapots.

my father tells me—

all rain that falls in Bosna
flows into the Black Sea &
every storm that shakes
Hercegovina bleeds into
the Adriatic (only he says
this in Bosnian, says
kiša, pada, oluja, voda)

he tells me that our river
is the Neretva & points a
vague north to where our
rijeka is born, traces a sketch
of her course through the
air & tells me I can swim
her to Hrvatska, to the sea

he takes me swimming
where she peels herself
into Jablaničko jezero,
shows me the streamlets
that race by our house to
meet her, and the pipes that
lead her back to rush

ice cold from our tap

my father tells me—

each drop that spills over
Perth is a precious thing
in need of saving for the
parched earth, the listless
wheat and fire-hungry
bush, the cloudless future,
& all the coming thirst

he tells me that this river
is the Swan, that she is
not ours but something
taken and awash in blood,
hemmed in and straining
& the least we can do is
let the grass go brown

he takes me swimming
where salt crusts our
limbs, dries in crystals
across uneven tides and
explains to me the power
you need to turn the sea
fresh, make her run sweet

& warm from our tap

My Mother's Keeper | HUDA FADLELMAWLA

I am my mother's keeper
And at five-years-old I learnt the importance of decorating
because I knew to move that pot plant to cover the blood stains
from you striking her the night before.

And I learnt that love sometimes can be the most harmful thing
because you give somebody all the tools to hurt you
and trust that they don't.
At five years-old, people's arms became the scariest place for me to run to
because the man that my mother dedicated the rest of her life
would use her as a vessel for his frustration and anger.

 I learnt that redecorating meant changing those
worn-out pillow sheets that caught her tears every night
when she walked into her bedroom broken
and that bedroom felt like crime scenes in each corner
and there are stains I have to wash away
so that when she awakes at
two o'clock in the morning screaming
afraid that she is not here anymore
because he hit her one time too hard.

I know what it's like when a bed shakes
and it isn't because love used to live here
It is because the bed has caught my mother's body too many times
when she's crashed into it.

And I've used my hands as bandages
And I've reminded her that her beauty and her courage
That a woman's body doesn't just expand to carry a life
That she is like a body of armour that has kept her protected
because she has caught so many hits to her chest
and still remains here.

I am my mother's keeper
Because I've witnessed crimes from the ages of five to ten
and she stills stands strong

So when she packed a suitcase when I was ten
and wrapped everything that she is
and flew all the way here
I knew what it was like when a woman
had to staple a smile on her face
and use her eyes as a welcome mat.

For the world to see that there are scars
that live on her back
that I rub every night
to remind her that those scars will bend
into the letters of the alphabet.
And I will write 'I love you' on each world
And remind her that she had created royalty out of her statistics
that the only thing that would ever live in a shopping list was poverty.

I am my mother's keeper
Because you have taught me
that no matter how many times the world beats you
you will get up.
And your knees are tired of dragging everybody
who is broken behind you
That true love is not chasing people
Because it sometimes just feels like we're running away from loneliness

I am my mother's keeper
I love you

Native Grasses | JEANINE LEANE

Native grasses
have got to watch their backs
be careful where they put their heads up
nobody wants
them
on their property or in their garden

people call them pests
try to kill them off spread poison
pull them out by their roots
you get fined for having too many of
them
if you let them grow
they spread like wildfire all over the country
seeds in the wind

you'll lose control
they'll
take over the other story you're planting
under roses privets irises and wheat fields
no introduced species has a chance
against a stand of natives so
they
get exterminated crushed buried under concrete
blown up eradicated

native grasses
they keep getting in the way of progress
you
need 90% of them destroyed to show
you own this place now
there are fines if you let too many of
them
live and flourish and rewards
if you can kill them all

still
we come back in small spaces
all over the place in
cracks in pavements respectable gardens
manicured lawns wheat paddocks golf courses
school playgrounds and all other places
we're
not wanted us native grasses
we've got to watch our backs
we
keep trying to raise our heads.

elephants guzzle a stash of corn wine and snore on a field
in Yunnan, while this time elsewhere, la niña begins, and in Australia,
my mother's lungs fill with rain, as ministers argue over how to divide
a river, I bring her meals, wash my hands for 20 seconds afterwards,
parliament discusses whether they should mine under our supply
of drinking water, I sanitise the counters with Dettol wipes, register
their deliberations, her face so young behind an N95 mask, but no
one questions the future of our bodies, Filipino women die
so heroically, our nation's infinite natural resource, the doctor
comments she doesn't need a large dosage for my mother's
"tiny" frame, at 8pm, everyone stands on their balconies to clap
for healthcare workers, applause smattering the gloom with useless
detonations, reminding the pigeons of private property,
but don't worry, *nature is healing*, a viral meme says,
humans are the real virus, researchers say they don't yet know
the long-term effects of January's smoke, PM 2.5 lingering
in the bloodstream, leading to heart disease, diabetes, dementia,
by her bedside, I stow inhalers in dependable plastic, our own
futures up for debate, but the elephant story was fake,
the dolphins in Venice, too, their sparkling heads
photoshopped into the dross of canals,
their true routes remote from the fact
of our bodies, essential even
when not at work, taking
all the air needed
to float

I am watering myself in the dark. I am pulling the hairs out of my throat one by one. This is how I look for cavities. When a hair is broken at the end it is a fracture in the consciousness of the skull it grew from. If a hair sits still in the throat, it will reincarnate as a soapy fish. If it writhes like a wavy crêpe paper snake, it is neither here nor there, like an artist or philosopher. If it pulls out easily, it wants to overthrow the government.

Every time we laugh, paper birds fly out of our mouths, and out the open window, and into the pink air, and into the realm of the flowers.

We are swimming in the milky watercolour pond. Tadpoles are flowering into frogs. The frogs are growing old but not aging. We are eating lilies the way we always do in dreams. They taste like nothingness leaking from the void from which we were birthed. I am pulling the hairs from my throat and grating them into our flowers for more flavour. I want more flavour because I need confirmation of my existence. I want more flavour because I am insatiable. I want more flavour because I am never happy with what I have. I want to put the world down my throat. I want to feel it orbit inside me with my hairs and my lilies and my paper birds. I want more than I need. I want to talk and I never want to listen. I want to take and I never want to give. I am grating my hair at 80 BPM.

The truth about flavour is that it cannot exist unless there is a snake shaped rhythm which can serve as a backbone for the meaning of life. Tadpoles only flower into frogs when the waters are singing in C major.

The lilies we eat open their mouths and say,

'KNOWLEDGE IS OBSOLETE. THE BIRDS OF PEACE ARE OBSOLETE. THE FROGS OF PEACE ARE AN OCTAVE TOO LOW. TIME IS MOVING BACKWARDS. TIME IS OBSOLETE'.

The lilies are lying.

I am milking my lungs in the watercolour light. We ate the lilies without asking their permission and now they are disseminating mistruths and double meanings in our bellies. I learned how to love in One-Dimensional world in a One-Dimensional way. I learned how to love not by being a writer but by being a chameleon. I am a chameleon who sits in one tree and changes colours. I am a chameleon who always has a new face. I am not a writer. I am a stranger. I am a Theremin. You cannot see my sounds but you can feel them with your tongue, your fingers and your feathers. I am not a writer. I am a Mirror. I only exist so you can see yourself. I am not a writer. I am a Lyre. I am a demon. Twice, demons came for my life. This is because I share their lineage.

The lilies we ate share our lineage.

I DRAW A WINDOW IN THE SKY TO ALLEVIATE MY NAUSEA. I VOMIT A CIRCLE OF FRACTURED HAIRS INTO THE MILKY POND.

Through the window is a cluster of shimmering aluminium foil stars that we cut out and pasted in the sky when we were children. The frogs open their mouths. They go in one by one then two by two. The window will only let you in if you have grown old but not aged. I have aged a thousand years. But I have become younger. We are moved by the transcendence of the frogs. We cry and cry.

Every time we cry, winged paper snakes grow out of our eyes, and into our yellowing mosquito nets, and into the tin foil sky, and into the realm of windows.

THE FROGS OF PEACE ARE AN OCTAVE TOO LOW. OUR CONSCIOUSNESS IS A CHARLATAN. Like the lilies in our bellies and the hairs in our throats and the paper birds and paper snakes that grow from our laughter and our tears. Our fractured catacombs will be put back together by frogs and played like instruments. I will play you and you will play me. And we will be born.

New Year's Eve Eve | EMILY STEWART

I'm not the only mammal living here
        the question is

 star achiever
            enduring theme

I've swapped cheese for nutritional yeast
                now if you could

 friends with benefits movie
            develop the courage to ask her

 where is the cyclone
            who is in the hammock

 easy and natural conversationalist
            take into the next world

the banned Iranian director Jafar Panahi
                the original idea

 the secrets I know about my friend's friends
            I see them occasionally at the cinema

malatang dinner
                        where you choose

Gramsci and Keats, the graveyard in Rome
            the new coronavirus

 Pomodoro technique
            turn right down Rose St past the tennis courts

enough water for three days
                it wasn't a perfect film

 no *Rosemary's Baby*
            what did you learn this year

how to ocean swim
         ethical banking

 next visit I'll
                  say hi and pass on my love

pottery
         am I on shaky ground

 which bad habit did you kick
                           is that q too private

ACAB, ATIAB
         serenade me

I want to believe the wombat shares its burrow
                  there was a cigarette box on Gramsci's grave

 my modest savings
         what do you know about grime

I smoked one of them
         tiredness in the extreme

 I gave the money to a family member
                  they're not the ones

looking for the right
                  1970s glass bead curtain

 it will take an enormous amount of water
         I gave the money to a friend

to mix the concrete
                  to build the wind farm

loudly
      if we move the holiday period

the colour of sand
      being ordinary

small, dead marsupial
      in an ALDI shopping bag

social fever
      floating floor

say the same thing back at me
      through the mirror

there are plenty of other problems
      that person deserved to get dragged

comms person
      this anger

insistent rhythm
      ziggurat

say the same thing back at me
      guessing

say hi arid love!
      Keats's grave was in a charming position

take into the next world
      that major theorist. no

fold down the sofa
      I'm searching for practical advice

old horror, new horror
      slip up, speculate and roam

total stocktake of foibles

cute clash—lemon and violet

I'll sip at your drain
                    counterstrike

there is great wisdom, beyond intellect
            counterstrike

I'm entering a more hopeful period
                        counterstrike

but for the dimming world
                bouillon

itchy
        alive

invoking the letter of the law
            a hand-drawn map

it will get worse
                        in what small way

can I help
        my beautiful father

rainfall
            non-violent direct communication

take a deep—'self-care poem'—breath
            dinner party feat. Jerusalem artichoke

trying every day to cast irony aside
                    the tone of the interviewer

don't ask me to formulate a jury
            an effect simply morphs

its form evolves
		young talented baker

charmless lawyer
			weekend hiker

buttressed
			is it blowing over

breathing the same air
		rising dough

bird book left by the ridge
				initials on every page

cracked windscreen
		Eton mess

I walked across that river you like
		the epithet

guitar solo
			a nice place to be

lie on the grass
		at the top of the salary range

she is whole
		still without power

tent and annexe
				pieces of the puzzle

admonitions
			sate my hunger

undo grammar
                              vulnerable position

climb the fence
              love what you do

move towards forgiveness
                              stingers beneath

  dreary little interior
              a clean soul

if it's supernatural it's not reality
              surround sound

  hailstorm
                              money tree

I'm cosy in my second body
              swimming cap

  send for help
              retreating further and further away

sing the phrase badly
              watermark

what day is it
              thrillseeker, orientation

  in the open air
                      open-air…

linen sky
              alphabet

lying on the floor
                    handsomely

gossip
          not chipboard, polished concrete

an eloquent cough might save us
                              limited shade

so willing to confide
              the spirit of the system

debut
                    loading up on groceries, bags and bags

the edge that is softest
                    a gummy edge

prose afternoon
            a sharp, sharp pencil

the architecture of the rose
                        recipient of a long generous letter

cutting the secret
            every mark so well drawn

terrible glare
            forthright

follow your interests
            aerobic activity

protected from the wind
                    smiling eyes
large cactus
            dress-code

sweep, knot
　　　aura or shadow

　aromatic
　　　　　idea for a character and scene

hidden clause
　　　　earring, blood-sport

　tacking out the pattern
　　　　principled

city and suburb
　　　hibiscus iced tea lemon & mint

replace a door
　　　　　　away from the countryside

　the sorrows of young Werther
　　　　faddish

that feeling of excitement
　　　　Casio beat

　this will be remembered
　　　　reproduction pinned on the wall

theatrical sleeper
　　　　　　fluttering

tennis welcome

　　　okay earth

we knew leisure, not catastrophe
　　　　the production of overtime

aggressor
　　　uploaded to academia

I'll tell you what happened
                terrible argument

model citizen
                pass—fail

reimagining wealth
            texting

I was in trouble but I was allowed my story
            going for a run

comprising argument and evidence
            picking up your rubbish

driving slowly, parallel to the main street
            fibro emotion

furnished bedroom
                untangled cords

climate change handbag
            relaxed

I barely know which question, or what is—
            a question

today is a leap day
            I saw there was a diagram on the tree

eyes lighting up
                it was likely that x substance

just quietly
            pose savassana

my climbing vine won't climb
            Hume Highway

that's what you get
      the complete breakdown

world health
      choir power

we killed an hour
            trial period

here in my chest
      small brushstrokes create texture

such enigmatic torpor
      my metier

haptic
      tit for tat

world id
            the community's roaming fauna

I'll go along with it
      a midnight fantasia

seeking comfort
      human and impressionable

next gen
            the legendary wall of sound

No Matter How Much Skin I Lose I Am Always the Same Body
| *HEATHER TAYLOR-JOHNSON*

I was shedding, stripped and blue-veined. It happens every few years,
each time an earnest battle. I don't like war metaphors. I was sick,
which led to the first backrub. I remember discussions of tin roofs,
no heat like Adelaide-heat and mimosas, flowers when a friend died.
I was reading a lot of grunge then, illness a new kind of sloughing,
an ecdysis. I bled. There were dogs, the park at midnight and when you
said you were falling in love with me I asked if I had to move out.
We kissed by the garden where carrots struggled under a dead
grapevine. There was acquiescence then, later wisteria, my skin
trailing behind us and you tripping over it. For a second I thought
we were in this together. You bathed me. There was ginger
in everything we ate. There was a couch that unfolded into a bed
which I lay on for aching hours while you went out into the world.
I wrote poems about sex and chilli peppers. When the winter rain
hit Adelaide we talked about tin roofs again. I'd grown new skin
that you liked to touch. It covered my body, which was mine.

When I am asked to visualise a meadow,

I think of the one

from Howl's Moving Castle.

More than any other year this was the year of starting things and not

      finishing them.

Buy seeds only to not plant them. Buy plants only to not water them.

All those TV shows where the murderer was society all along.

All those unheard songs

only to crawl back to the familiar.

Lately, my lessons have been learning me.

I tell the doctor I sleep well enough and tomorrow comes regardless.

I say I am yearning for a place I've never been

and that I am learning to cope

by learning to paint and learning to breathe.

From my belly.

Emerged a deep purple wave. A full circle.

On a walk, I see the street full of people enjoying spring. Remembering spring

is the season where plants shiver new seeds into soil, then await the

      right conditions.

Every day, both despair and hope sit on my shoulders and

make me dance,

news cycle by news cycle.

The spring rain left puddles. Puddles holding all I know

about suburbia. Her lights. Street lamps. Amber, like cat's eyes.

I'm sorry

I have called today and many days

similar to today, 'hell on earth'.

In my defence,

it felt

and feels

like a terrible train ride, one where after working long hours on my feet,

I then stood the whole way

and had nothing

to hold onto and steady myself. On the train

a stranger

kept staring at me, then finally asked: *Are you okay?*

To which I remember replying, I AM, and believed it.

On finding Charlotte in the Anthropological record
| *JUDITH NANGALA CRISPIN*

We meet on the surface of a photograph, as a fish and bird might meet in a lake, at a point of sky and the water's plane. Charlotte, in a book called *The Aborigines of Northern Victoria*, sits jade-black on earth, wind disarranging her hair. Trees obscured by falls of campfire ash. Her nudity is covered by a blanket. I don't know if her breasts are hanging, if her thighs bear designs or marks. A needlework of scars crosses her chest, repeated dots, like patterns on a goanna's back, like rain spat by goannas into dirt. Soon constellations will appear over branches, on this night of ninety years ago, this never-again night—and she asks me: "Where did you go girl, with your made-up history, your ever whiter babies?" This is what remains, a record of relatedness—scars to hold the memory of someone precious after they've died. We begin by cutting skin—rub wounds with gum and ash, black ants to cauterise the flesh. I remember them telling me: don't worry, this blackness fades with each generation. Charlotte is a map of a Country stained by massacres: Skull Creek, Poison Well, Black Gin's Leap. A geography of skin and land—maps for the returning, for those who speak only a murderers' tongue, whose songlines are erased, who consulted departments of births, deaths and marriages, who stood beside rented Toyotas, clutching photographs, in a hundred remote communities, asking strangers "Do you know my family? Can you tell me who I am?" This moment, an old light is crossing the boundaries of emulsion, and I say to her—Charlotte, Grandmother of my Grandfather, I am Judith, and these are my scars.

The Ordinary Poem | URSULA ROBINSON-SHAW

after Sean Bonney

there is a place more real than desire
as real as a train or a brick or a sarcoma,
words are cleaner there, swaying whitely
like feathers in warm air, where dignity
whispers like silk skirts. in the place,
every thing is a thing in comparison:
all bodies are dancers, all objects are symbols,
all symbols are monuments

in the place, poems are money,
money is credit, credit is debt, debts are futures,
futures are the everyday. all items are accounted for. and this
puts the prophets out of business...

more real than desire is a train,
the view from the glass streaked cheaply with shapes —
overgrowth, flickers of bare life, smoke screens, blackened
scaffolds stark as nudity, satellites in the eaves,
leaden feet shuffling —
through the glass, all monuments are symbols
all bodies are a right hand

on a train, cold as a cistern, i write a list of demands:
i demand a new textual violence,
the restoration of the slap and the blow with the fist,
a recession of dailiness,
a cultural shift, the resensitisation of horror,
i demand vitriols, gentle words falling away like stewed meat until a slump
in loveliness becomes a long, low hum,
i demand futures become threats, right hands become fists,
i demand the bright morning arrive, sparkling and odious, i demand
the names of every motherfucker who looked
at the heaving earth and saw an outcome, a teacup or a clean line,
the decorous rhythms of greenhouse plants,

every motherfucker who said there is a place
more real than desire, this is a debt-soaked world, the universe
lawfully unfolds, on this side
cast depravity as labour, cast the decadent as worker, consider the grindstone
in its manifest beauties, the drones in the ceiling, their celestial tones, find
bells, the sun, angels,
all worn to nubs, wrest them from the dross
with peace and honour, birdsong,
winter tomatoes tart and bitter, the happiness of bread, barbarity knitting a
        sweater, no —

i demand all bells become feral, i demand the sun
and gnashing angels, i demand knives and needles, elegance laid down on the
        rails, visions,
i demand all vulgar words become flesh, fuck the state, fuck debt, cops,
        collectors,
enforcers, collaborators, bon mots, fuck the novel fuck it all until the air is
        thick with demands
and in the dark recall the guillotine is not a symbol, not a monument
it is as real as a train
as a brick as a sarcoma, real as your right hand

Shaping shell through sentiment in sediment,
something like an initiation into   *blood love*
unbroken

//

Across the oceanic Country that is
                silver of salt of mother tongue
            to the place where you always are
        there is a   relic   beneath the water
    which is also a   relic   in itself

//

I will give you an oyster
to press the softness against your heart,
        to sense the ebb of sharp edge against salted skin
            and watch the purple rind change under moonlight

//

If a grain of sand has relived the myth
and become a pearl, iridescent
                behind shy oyster walls not yet ajar,
        then I will extract the myth from the stars
                            and give you

                                    a pearl,
over and over again,
                which is to say
                    I will give you my heart.

Poem whose semiotics of arrival | SHARI KOCHER

in Bogan Town make a perfect
O-shaped hair doughnut peeling
off the scream with an interior

brush inside four windowless walls
(narrow-doored servant quarters)
in which you nurse a pair of llamas

with long-lashed eyes whom I met
as dolphins when you leapt from the dock
into their dreams braving the dirty

foam-wracked waves without volition
as they swam into you to sup
as llamas on human milk

their sorrow part of whatever they sought
still dolphins at heart, shapeshifters
who had foreseen beyond this dream

the draining of their sea. Fully awake
then for your first day of work in polo
shirt and tights, I am met

by a man beside your car
whipping a tree with his belt,
his visage a violent stew—

and you burn my fingers getting into
the car as his voice lays into two
small daughters on the curb in mini-

school skirts and bows, struck
to the quick that they must follow
this shout, who marches off

without looking behind him
a pulse of hot concrete forcefully
threading his belt back in.

Pool Boy | DALEY RANGI

he called me   *pool boy*
due to my   ambiguity

               not quite white
               not quite not

                           despite

my presence

as if i *should*
by virtue of exxxotikah
"tidy up"

               after them
               before them
               serve them

grasping my net tight
collecting   sundry   debris
from   clinical   holes (in which)
nothing   may   flourish
but them

i will do this for you
(an honourable occupation—slave to summer sojourns)
drip   my   golden   sweat
bend   my   bronze   beauty

make l a b o r i o u s love to your faux concrete lagoon
if only you would reach for a net too
if only you would clean *my* ocean
nothing ambiguous about that,   *ocean boy.*

I translate roses as multiples, a rose and a rose and a rose

I paint all my corners different colours

I welcome my own redundancies, and all that time to kill

I resurrect the dead for a second when I close my eyes

I slide that agnostic load from my shoulders in a flash of unearthing

I face east then west to respect my indirection

I swallow the moonlight and hope it may ward off the sincere and
      embarrassing shadows I've shed

I return to multiples

I alphabetise my dreams hoping for order

I set fire to my opinions and wait for the truce

I find lost amulets in the gutter left by cyclists or the stars and bless them
      again with unchained secrets

I strike light into the dark passage where the summer moths return

I forget my body is what I have with me until my fingers and breath do
      their work

I tinker with the time it takes to remember

I remember everyone I forgot

I promise the invisible I will return one day

I lean against the transcendent, listening to the honeyeaters fight in
      the camellias

I talk to absence like the one who has gone

I ask emptiness to fill me

I deface all my damage because the world won't forgive me

I recite a history of my own breath, which is the poem

The Roaring Twenties | LIAM FERNEY

UM—YEP—NO.
You don't get the kind of war you deserve
you get the kind you get.
A white van man van with no man melted at Yatte Yatah.
The peach stand spared.

Don't fret. We thought of everything.
We packed lions for the evacuation centre.
Astonished clowns gurning to be fed.
Thank the circus for stumping up for juice
after the transformer's fire fritz.

Bless the carny with hot chips and dagwood dogs
for days enough to last this arc
of a prequel to apocalypse, say toodle-pip to glum teens
and good morrow to the roaring twenties.

Sandstone Academy | MYKAELA SAUNDERS

sandstone
cut up for construction of ivory towers
gouged out of soft homelands leaving deep wounds behind

ivory tower
fortress made of memory
imprisons our history and keeps us locked outside

fortress   panopticon of scrutiny   gazing out
at everything but never
looking
in

vultures
gorging on our culture
extract stories from people butcher both in the doing

experts   sneer as they teach about us
forging   wealth
and   reputations
from   a   syllabus   of   lies

anthropologists   dissect us and measure us
against   self-
given   standards
manufacturing   their   supremacy

scholars   mutilate our teachings
construct   them
as   myths
as   they   concoct   their   own

science
violates our sanctity
sanctioning perverted
hands molesting flesh and bones

buildings
named for
who
genocidal
of fascist
eugenicists
worshipped
fantasies
regimes

museum
prison house of
artefacts   consumes and
entombs us in grotesque displays

instructors
induct tomorrow's
leaders
in the uncivilised
traditions
of the colonising
country

innovators
of bureaucratic
violence
proselytising
theories
of our gentle
dying out

leaders   saviours
under pretence   doing the
of progress   lord's work
promoting   dislodge the bedrock
cruel policies   of culture
that pressure   thieving bubbies
our demise   from kin

academy   insists on its own humanity   as history's horror stories seep from porous stolen stone

173

Sandwiches | ZENOBIA FROST

when the orderly comes to take the tray of sandwiches Dad can't possibly eat
I am compelled by an impulse to eat the sandwiches and also to catalogue them
for a later poem that I know I will write / here is the poem 20 months later
led by the mock pulse of throaty lungfuls / hot air / I want to eat the sandwiches
because they are there and free and I have trained myself to fill up
on hors d'oeuvres in a crisis / a blanket over the vinyl chair says HEALTH
which seems ironic and funny and I want to take a picture of the blanket but I wait
until everyone is out of the room / I want to take a picture of Dad but I don't
because I am ashamed / as a child I had to dig up my fish in their matchboxes
from under the petunias just to check / I always knew this would be a big poem
because of the way the room ballooned / my aunt nervous because Dad
didn't want anyone to see him like this / not even me / Mum Janette Bec Aunt
me Dad / that's not that many until the nurse folds in the trundle bed / what
my aunt means is why is my girlfriend there / imagine being in the first breath
of love and meeting her dad already unconscious / a few days later meeting her
entire blood / welcome to the family / I would rather Aunt stayed out / so performative
with an arm over mum wailing / I get a minute alone and I am like Dad *let me tell you*
about the giant stingrays overhead / can you see them? / we're going round and
round the tunnel at the aquarium / all the moray eels popping their heads out
to say bye / I tried to sing 'Dangerous' by Roxette but I couldn't / I needn't
have worried about sandwiches because Janette has made a tonne / Janette is stalwart
and practical and when she makes you sandwiches you eat them / this is a love
I can understand / hi to Graeme & Janette from this poem / a couple of days before
I'd put Dad's socks on his cold feet / if I am honest I didn't visit hospital much
because my parents were always there taking turns / hospital was our summer house /
I thought Dad would light up when I told him I'd started boxing but he didn't
so I was a sullen teen again / his only question was *when are you going to learn*
to drive so I thought I'd get my license while he was getting better and then *ta da* /
people started saying *ask your Dad lots of questions about his life* but he never asked
about mine / Dad loved to have a cheese-and-Branston Pickle sandwich at like 11pm

and then complain to Mum about buying carbs / I hold my breath when my aunt calls down the hall where I am dozing with a sandwich / a doctor comes in to call time and the nurse snips at him for not taking off the oxygen mask / it is 10.45pm so close to sandwich hour / she calls Dad *sweetie / okay sweetie /* a surprise breath / *it's all right* / Aunt starts asking Dad's spirit to fix the lotto in her favour / *sweetie* / soon I will make many phone calls and discover all the ways people react to bad news / I didn't realise how quickly it happens the body changes like *that* / one second it just wants me to drive and then it can't eat the sandwiches

You   lead   me   down   to   the   ocean.
I   tell   you   I   know   a   little   about   currents
but   nothing   about   open   water.   We   are   not   holding
hands,   but   we   are   close   despite   the   rip.
There   is   a   trench   and   soon   you   are   up   to   your   waist,
as   I   tentatively   dip   my   chicken   feet
into   the   cold   Autumn   soup.
There   are   so   many   bad   poems   about   the   sea.
You   are   not   a   bad   poem   about   the   sea.
I   stand   on   the   shore   of   this   dream,
there   is   plastic   everywhere   within   me.
How   do   we   recycle   that   which   was   never   used
or   broken?   You   lead   me   down   to   the   ocean.
You   say   -   there   is   the   break.   Here   is   the   wave.
There   is   where   the   sand   covers   up.
Here   is   the   line   and   the   hook   of   a   lip.

There the disappearing horizon.

Simaetha | GIG RYAN

(Idyll II, Theocritus)

Where are my bay leaves and charms, my bowl with crimson flowers
while he inexorable
has gone from my bed like a dress
Distance: spells of fire wreathe you

Shine on this spin or grave
as sight stunned me

leaves burn
Wheel of brass turning from my door

Now wave is still and wind is still
My heart stopped in its foundry

As horses run, so we to it
Starts love's knife

whose hair shone like dunes
whose body greased with labour

He had brought apples and his hair sprigged
unasked love into the oak and elm

and words went and came
Now from my lintels

Day drags from me and tells his flowers elsewhere
Farewell, ocean and its team,
whose white arms wrap
Silver flute who sang, and bright-faced moon
who knocks on a door of shadows

A rose for you, to match the wound
but tomorrow's like now

N.B. Lines 1, 8 and 9, see Theocritus Idyll II, 'The Greek Bucolic Poets', translated by J M
Edmonds, Loeb Classical Library, Harvard University Press, 1912.

Spare keys | RICO CRAIG

In the future my daughter will love
and that will be enough. Blood will flow
under her skin. The hounding daily news
will be a source of fleeting fear. She will

concoct plans to upend this world. Her friends
will message too much, they will carry discontent
far into the future; it will be temporarily
glorious. We will say goodbye through car windows

as we rush to other people and places—and it will
be enough. Every message she sends will be
without punctuation, and if I read them closely
they will run together, they will be a procession

of days, and, even a single word will be enough.
One day she will come to me asking for spare keys
to her flat. I'll find them in my drawer,
we'll walk over to her place. On the way we'll

talk about the nights we spent bound to bad
television, waiting for B-listers to reveal scores.
Really we'll be talking about something else,
we'll be saying—I'm well. How are you?

We'll be hovering around each other
with memories. I'll be using my right hand
to shade the sun, she'll be wearing sunglasses,
and it will be enough to pretend I'm too lazy

to walk up her stairs. She'll appear at the window
above and call my name. I'll edge around and wait
for her to drop the keys in my hands. Cars will
pass on the street behind me. This will be

true and possible. She will wave from the window,
she will say—see you later. A bus will pass,
somewhere a tree will grow new leaves—
uncountable trees and their uncountable leaves,

learning to live again, learning to fill us
with their air. I will wait, looking up
as she draws back through the open window.
I will think of the endless shades of green,

all the edges of leaves, fronds, needles
making their way into the world, and it will
be enough, it will help us to breathe.

Still Life | JINGHUA QIAN

Remember that year we sat in the stench of death,
peering at lighted squares, searching for the numbers of fallen.
I was conscious of my breath, conscious of the too-close bodies
passing in the aisles, conscious of the skin of the oranges,
already touched, in the pile. I tried to grieve,
I tried not to cough. I couldn't sleep or I slept too much.
I tried to believe that words were enough, but I wore
them through. There was nothing to do, or everything to do
and no one to touch. It was a communal crisis of the flesh
yet I lost mine in the wash, lost sense of the seasons
and the earth and the feeling of the turn as the world shrank down
to assorted squares of sound and sight.
We joked that none of us would age that year. A desperate lie
while op-eds sneered that it wasn't worth a dollar
to save people from dying if they were already old.
All life was cheap, some was cheaper.
All bodies are material, only some matter.
The killings were watered down, the victims rewritten
as if they were already dead or dying.

Even back then, we knew our bodies
were sacred, our inheritance lush,
our ancestors attentive. I carried
the strength of my lineage,
I learnt to shed its burden.
The gift was wheat but not bread,
fruit but not wine.
In those days, the bosses and their machines
stole our time. They crept into our houses,
they owned our faces and stories
and footsteps and grammar and sold them on.
All that our ancestors gave us,
the market clambered to purchase, trade,
perfect and erase. We fought back,
marching in the streets, singing in the towers,
bleeding on film and paper. It wasn't enough.
The water climbed up, the fires burned hotter, the prisons

swelled and swallowed more of our number.
The second summer of that year indoors,
the old world came knocking and flirting again.

Wheat but not bread. Fruit but not wine.
We had to take our time back, hold close
to the skin of the earth, feel the turn inside and out.
There was no script, only the noise at the door
and an ache in my neck and a dim memory
that once we were worth more.
There was no blank page. No empty land.
Never a moment that felt like the stage was set
for the world to come. There was only the unmarked seed,
the garden already overgrown, and between the weeds and flowers
there was work—there was living to be done.

STORY TREE | *ALI COBBY ECKERMANN AND JOY HARJO*

Ali, Sister—

I lay my body down. My mind does not slow for sleep. It has no place to rest,
Not in this country, this government, this time of the heavy turning earth.
An eternity can exist in a moment, an hour, or in the song life of the humble
sparrows who mutter as they dream in the tree that breaks through concrete and
sorrow of this poem.

Five trains cross the city.
The man chased by demons screams out. He roams this area day and night.
His bad dreams never sleep. They beg our ears for mercy.
A ruined goddess dressed in streetlight begs a ghost for change.
She wears a crown of cigarette smoke.

Tulsa is the corrupted form of our name for "town" or "old town":
Tallasi, or *Tvlvhasse*.
Down the street the ashes of the fires we left behind in the forced march
Were rekindled beneath the Council Oak Tree. It is still there: our story and
The tree who holds it in place, and the memory of fire.
The thieving never ends. And now the pandemic haunts us Indians, takes us,
Especially those of us who are older. In our Mvskoke culture
Elder is respected. In the swallowing-everything-up culture, we are
death watch.

Those viral killers approach my mind to plant fear. They act familiar, shake hands,
make treaties. They sit down without being invited. We recognize them as part of
the great disturbance.

I give my mind the task of holding the door open for the ancestors, the guardians,
the winds. When I sing there is no way in for evil.

Once in the middle of the country in the early of my life, I drove my children
through the night in our small pickup truck, back from a winter break in Tulsa,
north to my education, my way out. We stopped for gas.

Cold winds had blown and blasted us for hours. Snow was now drifting the highway.
My son jumped out to clean the windshield.
My baby girl stood up and yawning, she said:

"I was just dreaming someone somewhere else, and I wonder if someone
Somewhere else was dreaming us."

Then she went back under the sleep blanket and drifted to where she had come from—to the origin place of poetry, the eternal road between your people and mine, between you and me.

We filled up, kept driving through the darkness.

My girl became a dreamer with her beadwork
Her designs emerge from father-mother ancestor patterns as her children and grandchildren play around her.

And my son labors on the railroad, always moving, leaping agile to the next thought of history on the tracks of living. He worked on each of these trains running through this city, just yards away from this room as they carry oil, coal, and other extractions from beloved earth, as his daughter takes the path of plant and animal knowledge.

Here we are on the verge of shift. We lost three culture-carriers within days. Others are on ventilators, turning toward the next sacred story.

I find myself in the night, which is your next day, reaching through
Eternal wonder, through the mind field of prayers, to you.

Everything is a prayer driving, singing, crying, falling down, getting back up, the small animals that we meet on the road, the trees, the beingness, the becoming.

You are a prayer, my sister.

Dear Sister

There are no trains here. The railway lines have been removed, the station house vacant in disrepair. I wait by the broken platform for my son's return. There is no view of him. I no longer knows where he lives.

Millions of trees are demolished to build the railroad. Now barely a tree survives. You and I know old trees hold memories. It is tragic these trees have been destroyed. No factual re-telling of first contact is encouraged here. So much is denied when truth hangs dismal in the air.

Miles of empty railway corridors are re-sown with native seeds, the regeneration of saplings an offering to the native animals and birds, a haven built by those who have destroyed what was. Of course I am excluded. I am no longer fauna and flora. There is no returning. There is no re-turn. Truth is a lonely weight to carry.

An urgency arrives on a crying wind. My grandmother lives there. She reminds me to walk. I turn and walk and walk and walk. I do not run. I feel hope dying on my breath. A thin ribbon of trees reveals hidden inside the horizon. My mother lives the sunset. My mother reminds me. This is the route to the river.

I wade into the water. I know you are here by the trees. I know everyone is here. Tall trees grow here. The girthed trees are the Elders. They remind me to rest. In the comfort of their shade I perceive my daughter. She lives here in the shadows unable to leave. She has become water that slows silent over sand. I follow her to the sedge grass. It grows strong here. I weave a dilly-bag to carry her. I weave a dilly-bag to carry us. I weave my way back through the mystery of time. I am footsteps in the sand.

I send you stories in my dreams. I read your stories in the leaves. I love our secrets. I have guarded mine since birth, my inheritance from my grandmother. A story-tree grows inside me and can only be viewed in my eyes. I remember you held me in your gaze. You know my secret. Now everything is secretive. Ask the birds.

On the platform I wait for my son. Roads crisscross where the trains once ran. I walk to the motorway. Our grasses do not grow here. Our animals lay dead by the roadside. It is the sacrifice of us for as far as the eye can see. It is the tactic of the government to halt the arrival of prayer. It is a desolate land barren of trees.

Your prayer arrives through the silence of dismay, dropped from the talon of an eagles' claw, winged from your window to mine, that has flown from your heart.

Joy. It is exactly what I need.

And truth.

**** **** **** **** ****

Let us sew dresses
So we look the same as we walk toward the sun

We will make them together of grasses and winds
We find along the river of time, made of smooth stone

Stripping the chicken | ELLA JEFFERY

Days later I remember
the hot chicken, how it slid

in its plastic bag as I drove home,
its louche smell filling the car.

It must have gone bad, I think.
I taste it anyway

and it is not so bad. I lift it, womb-wet,
from its sac of juice and fat.

I am tempted to hold it close
and invite it to hear my heartbeat.

Instead, I run warm water. I sluice
congealed fat from its body.

Then I strip its skin, cut the strings
that bind its legs in a modest twist.

Under running water the breasts curved
like two white leaves fall away,

and the darker sheafs of thigh-meat, pockets
of underside meat sometimes

called oysters which fit like a coin
on the tongue. Now only bones are left.

I am impressed by the crackling scaffold
of its body, how easy it is to break.

The sound of rib hitting sink
is simple and ambient.

Now only a soft mound of stuffing rests
in my palm, misshapen as a brain. I wash

and wash until it reveals
the tiny man whose voice I have always heard.

Now he says to me 'You have made me
so proud. Buy another.'

Suite of Powers | CHRIS ANDREWS

A lime drops, then a mandarin,
and it's the saraband of mass.

Who buys a dose of agonist
gets a free dopamine spike right away,
and it's the gabber of energy.

A courier ventures into a valley
of ginger-biscuit bricks,
a fragrant paper bag in his pack,
and it's the curtain call of glow.

A bollard is vanishing under moss.

Some brain wakes invaded:
it's the bindweed of resentment again.

A wall graffed overnight proclaims:
wolfy knows dr awkward's wonky flow.
Of course: it's the ocean of influence.

Kids in a grounded caravan
pry open a mutant rhythm cell,
and it's the earworm of autumn
burrowing into your memory.

A cube is lost in a sweet solution.

A pec-popper glides by on muscle wheels,
and it's the mallet of bass.

An insult thrown out in casual anger
becomes a part of the target,
and it's the buried flag of adamance.

Row upon row of servers hum,
hoarding data just in case,
where a field of Irish grass once blew,
and it's the plunger of energy.

At the clear heart of a shed full of mess
it begins: the minuet of repair.

A pod-cracking corella mob moves in,
cocking pink-rimmed eyes,
and it's the law of the lever, simple.

A woman lifts a rubber glove
to her lips like a bugle and blows.
Two fingers pop from the swollen palm,
and it's the reveille of sense.

That? It's the sound of the mountain
of ballast replenished. And that?
The tantalizing, wind-smudged melody
of your life played very far away
on the ocarina of time.

A glass reserves its shattering power.

A wire swings under a butcherbird,
and it's the ballad of mass.

SUPERPOSITION | GRACE LUCAS-PENNINGTON

Too many blacks goin around, thinkin they own the place

—an old problem.

Time was, they knew their proper place;
[*hard workers, the blacks*]
these days, can't go two steps without falling over one
[*theyre lucky we came here*]
telling us we're the problem
[*lazy goodfornothin*]
yep too many uppity, wont-stay-in-their-lane blacks
[*farmers? youvegottabefuckinkiddin*]

Here sits an edifice; a pulpit
raised of shears rumbarrels chains ships bullets theft and bloodred death
book-lined, velvet-curtained
veneered in an unctuous justice
samely coating all the lives adjoined.

Within a man sits tracing ghostly ink, revolution emergent
as if thrown, a hairshirt spirals
verdant, down now onto this stage
twixt the sombre stacks of once-trees, much unvisited.

The man stops stoops lifts the bristling bundle
now heretic, ascends a stair other hands construct
the remnant curtains part, there 'ICONOCLAST' spelled out in neon
tubing pulsing
'gainst a white white wall.

Tomes clasped chestward, he—our reluctant cynosure—speaks
voice rising

(*streetpunk academic mutiny / circle back
toward lost fecundity*)
standing, blinking manifest sunlight

palaces and towers shed birds like skin
crowds swerve, bend ears, listen:

(there was always life before you
as there is always life after you
you have never been the first, or only)

—an old story.

and like a tree dragged upright, this roar
shunts a world

somewhere deep stone stratum cracks, unfastens earth-strong membranes

wave functions   collapse
potentialities formerly certified stable   corrode   diffract cohere no more

certain stories are fences / certain stories are seeds

gauche bylines slop our troughs to brimming
[gonna destroy im]
adamant fencers clinging to zero-sum
[fabrication realhistory]
mainlining militant indignant feeds maddened erupt
[madeitup fraudster notfarmers]
a vague relentless clouding morass
[sowhatiftherewerehousesyoucouldntinventthewheel]
overwhelm civil semblance
[savages]

two positions, superimposed

[You can't just   rewrite   history]

from *Television* | KATE MIDDLETON

5.

I discovered a version of God when I woke
too early Sundays for cartoons: the *Hour*

of Power, its earnest pastels, dawned before
the television would cede neon and mayhem:

two hours later I'd have forgotten, but in
the antsy minutes of 6am alone I'd press

the carpet with impatience until the sermons
ended: I probably liked the music: maybe

that's why I was curious about the faith
my classmates held, though not curious

enough for conversion: I know they weren't
the televangelists *The Handmaid's Tale*

imagined: I haven't watched that show yet,
something I didn't realise would make me

feel apologetic: the book's Serena Joy in
my mind played by one of those faithful

women I watched on Sundays, though
I learned of Tammy Faye and Phyllis soon

enough: imagine the shock of Gilead for
Tammy Faye, the shock of being stripped

of glamour: Tammy Faye, all big hair and
glimmer eyes, mascara and bold lips, modesty

replacing glam, but at least not stuck in
handmaid red, in handmaid bonnet, in

handmaid anonymity: the cartoons, meanwhile,
love letters to another logic I still hold dear:

the giddiness of Looney Tunes, an antidote
for weight piled on by years: the rules of

Roadrunner still circulate: *the coyote must
be more humiliated than harmed*: me, as viewer,

still annoyed by Roadrunner's always-smug
veneer, always in sympathy with coyote's

manic, fanatic, heretic, gravity-afflicted heart

at first
I carried them
back to her
that pile
of old white bones
I found
in the pocket
of a river's meander
high in a dry
floodwater bend
a shoal of
ten thousand river stones
the marbling shade
of elder casuarinas
knots
of roots
& smaller stones
eddies of earth
patched by
grass

having stumbled
upon
a farmer's Boeotian
slaughterhouse
set back
from the river's
cascade
quarrel & din
a silent
place for a bullet
the infirm
& broken
cows
led down
from
the paddock above
shot then &

their
scattered white bones
sculpted
by the high
sun
moving through
bleached
horns & the dark eyes
of their
forebears

I had only
my own eyes
to see
small zones
here & there
old bones
where bodies
drop
over time
&
then
down a bit
a rust brown
hide
taut over hollow ribs
stuck out
jaw open

forgive them
sacred cows
white milk
blood
& hard-baked
shit
the hide arched
over bone
into

a fly-blown
temple

who
would forgive me
though
when I
looked around
wandered yonder
& found
a remote pile
of bones
away
by a tangled pomegranate
scattered
dry
old white bones
the
skull first
resting
forward of the rest
two
clean bullet holes
resonate
with a
deathly cool
refrain
in the solid
resting
brow
& in
the skull's wake
a wreck
of vertebrae & ribs
their empty
cacophony

who

would forgive me
if I
took them
with me
all the way home
& out into
the world's
wide
tomb

my fingers
ran
along the smooth
dead
bone
& in a crack
I saw your
break
all the darkness
held inside
& so
variously figured
I should
indeed
take the bones
back
as the cracked
darkness
shared
might resonate
between us

so then
I first held the skull
up
brushed off
leaf muck
put it
aside

& over
time
picked
over
the dead
made a small
fine pile
of the best bones
& then
held
the deceased's
naked clatter
in an
armful
picked
up the skull
with my
remaining
hand
& walked
back down river

I held
my cache of white
like a baby
by the
welling, turning
water
took a narrow
path
over rock
by the rapids
where the
river spilled
the story
witnessed
all the dead
danced &
cried
in the cataract

of death
reflected
in the transparent
glissade
of water
then I rested
at a wire
fence
pushed all the bones
beneath
& crossed a wide grass
paddock
tall
seed-heads
licking the bones
as I passed
down by another
pomegranate
thicket
& then by the river
again
down
a dark tunnel
of trees
beside
deep black water
blue sky
mirrored
dead leaves sailing
through
a gallery
of overhanging she-oaks
& gums
maiden-hair ferns
the water's
hushed
movement

I came up
from
the river
out from the tree
shadows
holding the baby
load of bones
the skull
& when
I arrived at the house
she said
how when at first
she saw me
walking
from the distant corner
of the paddock
she had
panicked in horror
thinking
I was carrying
a dead child
up from the
river

we
laughed at this
as I lay
the bones at her feet
with some
dignity
for the substantial
presentation
of the dead
and we
looked at them
wordlessly
eternally
not a child
just bones

it was Easter
so we had time
to begin
making all kinds
of new
conditions
found
an old
bicycle wheel
rim
& tied
the ribs in
a hanging
circle
for the wind
to reanimate
& hallow
as her break
grew
wider
darker
& for a while
I broke
alongside her
was perhaps
even broken
by myself
but

I kept the bones
whole
the whole time
in a box
I bore
from house
to house
over the years
the skull
always

nailed in the wall
above
my writing desk
the vertebrae
placed
delicately
on windowsills
& bookshelves
their
long thin arms
white
angelic souls
dead
wombs
full of the river's
echo
silent letters
on the book spines
unknowingly
radiant
that's how
there are still
all these
old
bones of mine
on my desk
on bookshelves
& today
after a dream
where I
measured out the years
in bones
laid out
one
after the other
I held
the same vertebrae
I brought up
from
the river that day

& in its dead
light weight
gravity
I knew in fact
after all
it was a child
all along
not a bone
we held between us
then but
a child of the hollow
centre
where love like
marrow
of the same
flesh & blood
grew & grew
by the altar
of our bones
&
when they broke
they all
dried out
a river of dark blood
escaped
into the atmosphere

& so now
all the bones
are empty
corridors of dust
the child
a pile of bones
offering
as it did
back then
to be nothing

Unrecognised | ANDY JACKSON

National Portrait Gallery, Canberra

At five, the doors click shut. Security
walks a final circuit and clocks off. The eyes
      of the prominent are lost in the middle distance

beyond office, sports field or studio. Hair and skin
of oil, watercolour, polymer, the reassurance
      of names everyone should know. Not ours—

we are without shelter, without conservation.
But they cannot keep us out. At dusk,
      white walls become grey, darken.

When it's safe, someone gives the signal.
From the coal-black cloakroom chiming
      with empty hangers, through a broken

shutter at the gift shop, from underneath
the doors of an out-of-service toilet, we emerge,
      move through the gallery as smoke

or pheromones. In the dim cool,
minute cracks in the canvas, paper, plaster,
      open like pores to breathe us in.

Morning, the first visitor examines
each portrait, as if trying to remember
      or forget. Something about that black scar

of paint, the dishevelled bed in the background,
soft fold of belly-flesh, or the polished glass
      from which his own face gazes back.

I will die in HTML on a cloudless autumn night, a night when
the moon shines as brightly as the magnolia's silver throats
heady in verbena foliage, a night when possums scramble in trees
like nights when I languish, falling asleep and waking in fright

to my solitary, abused life, that nobody knows, least of all poets.
And the screen will be so bright it burns the eyes of strangers
like the 1295 friends I've added on Facebook. A night when I am
harmlessly sexted by an acquaintance and the logarithm Tweets:

*Michelle Cahill is dead. She died with noise-induced hearing loss
triggered by #extreme #phone use, having suffered acutely from
#asphyxiation.* The switchgear box for my apartment will fuse,
causing it to fatally explode. Among charred artefacts I'm found

in my study, glued to my laptop, the screen on saver mode,
dried serum from my repetitively strained fingers— & this poem
sublime in its deferred state. Very likely it will be a Thursday night,
recycle bins crammed between the dim silhouette of parked cars.

My cousin and my niece will adjust their settings on social media.
Nobody will guess the password to deactivate my enduring account.
But after the autopsy, as my ashes descend into the cradling earth
a hacker parsing code will pause to memorialise my Facebook page.

Venery | FELICITY PLUNKETT

Was it my breath
in your mouth, your trace
I couldn't shake?

Were we set upon
the board: die
apple, snake—the old game?

Whose dream was it? Fog's
dream? Hooftaps'?
Dream of sinew and foam?

Was the brass
blast rounding sleep's
corner sport? Force?

Were my wet
teeth close as we ran
with hares, with hounds?

Whose meat, whose
musk in the fold
and roll of capture

churn and lurch? Who
won? Who laughed? Whose
blood was on whose tongue?

THE WALK | JUDITH BEVERIDGE

To ease a compressed nerve in my back I took a walk,
but soon I wondered if the pain killers had started to trip
nightmare neural circuits because I heard a flock
of lorikeets ballyhooing, the creek played over stones a tune
from a decrepit piano. I saw eucalypts spark like the electric poles
of dodgem cars, cockatoos spruik from skeletal branches,
crows were opening and closing their wings like flaps
into marquees staging freak theatre and kookaburras
sent up peals of corrosive laughter when a brush turkey
with a conjoined twin on its back, crossed the path to greet
an atavistic specimen of bush-rat whose deformities
bought a tear to my eye. Whatever the reason for the bush
turning into a gross floor show, the carnival barkers kept on.
Leaves flashed like cards in the crooked fingers
of gypsy fortune tellers, so I walked over a small bridge
to a clearing where a silver frog with a fetish for incandescent
insects sat with its long tongue glittering. I wondered
what menagerie it had escaped from, poor specimens
of biological rarity, and just then, an encephalitic butcher bird
swooped and severed the frog's tongue swallowing it like a dagger.
I know that pain is a window into the grotesque.
I know the mind can torture with both real and imagined
possession, but by then I'd had enough of disablement
and deformity presented as entertainment, worried that next
I'd see a purple echidna forced to swallow flames.
I found my way out by following clumps of orange fairy floss
webbed in trees as if carnival spiders had been hard at work,
or Harpo Marx and Lucille Ball had ripped out handfuls
of their hair. As I left the reserve, a dwarf pink pademelon
stroked its beard, readjusted its tricorne hat. It was holding
a Harpo Marx doll ventriloquizing *Al-A-Ga-Zam,*
Al-A-Ga-Zam, though the doll's mouth remained firmly shut.
Then it switched phrases: *lama gazal, lama gazal*
a near anagram. I yelled back *ptomaine,* a near anagram
of pantomime. The pademelon ventriloquized *pharma hoax*—
then *brat trump,* close anagrams of the doll's name
and of PT Barnum. I said sciatic nerve—it returned
craven nectaries. Then it yodelled, laughed, put the doll
in its pouch and tunnelled quickly into a patch of long grass.

Watching a Simulation of the Birth of the Universe Poem
| ANUPAMA PILBROW

I am repotting my little plants giving them some tasty compost
as a treat watering them in with a seaweed solution loving and
cleaning the terracotta in the sun feeling my body sweating
and my eyes are blinding in the afternoon light and I am putting
away my bag of soil and it is bursting in my face and I am accidentally
inhaling a lot of soil and I am having a shower and cleaning all the
soil under my fingers and scrubbing them and scraping out the
mucus from my nose and inspecting it looking for soil particles
and coughing and hacking into my hands so I can spread out the
expectorate on my palms and hunt through for any specks of
brown and I am feeling in my chest every breath thinking if I can
feel a tightness or any evidence of the dust that has gone in them
and then I am looking up Legionnaires Disease and I am thinking
about legionella and aspergillosis and and feeling afraid for my life
and thinking do I need to make an appointment with my doctor and
telling her that I inhaled quite a lot of soil and I am feeling my
throat and sinuses drying out and I am noticing every ache and
pain and gently panicking that I might die from gardening and how
everything carries some hidden risk of death even gardening and I
am also feeling awe and thinking fondly of how many living things
are everywhere at all and how delicate is my hold on life even the
bacteria on my own skin can kill me and I am thinking how even
when our species is gone (which will be soon) there will still be living
things everywhere and how comforting and how quickly life formed
on our planet and how enormous our universe is and how ordinary
my own life is where are the aliens are they living ordinary lives are
they afraid of death and then I am watching a simulation of the birth
of the universe and I am seeing the unmistakable evidence that
actually we are entirely alone in this giant expanse one single blip

of activity in a terrifying long timeline of total nothingness and when we are gone it will all be quiet and eventually the cockroaches and algae will be quiet too and it doesn't matter if it happens to me early because of legionella or not because suddenly I am feeling so sad and so lonely that in so many billions of years really we have seen nobody else but our own earthly kind.

Waves | *JOSIE/JOCELYN DEAN*

You go to the beach
more than writing.
You undress
struggle yourself into
wet suit. You are hairless
smooth as suntan
lotion (like it, you
come off in water).
You filter
a whole sea
through the tongue.
You don't wear goggles,
taste of marine life/an eaten
7/11 bag on lips/teeth.
When a huge wave picks you
up, rolls you over onto back
like a cat in a washing
machine, you cackle, feel
naked. A trickle
of blood leaks
merrily. Stormy days
you tumble awing
at the Godzilla-scale
of waves: your unknowing protector.
You look underwater, the bottom
five bodies down.
You observe sun
caking your belly, a hundred sharks trans-
fixed in the waves. You feel
your body lightening
gills breaking out
feet forgotten/slaked/selkied.

What happens to books right now?...this begins with rationalisation of libraries...books get thrown out...put in the tip...they admit...the sacred book is gone... bookshops disappear...what happens here?... you tell me that ...the fresh smell of paper that would greet...that beautiful feeling of adventure ...and variety...all sorts and kinds ... hundreds and thousands...a treasure trove...Aladdin's cave...my childhood LIBRARY...I learn how to read here...that long time... extended...submersion immersion...imagine it all... focus...now the discount store...the remainder...the sale ... the second hand bookstore vanishes...what do I do with my books? I put them under my bed... and books ...here are ideas...I teach.. I will expand a world...but now a shrinkage...a silence...a quieting down...a contraction now...the library goes online...but it uploads books nevertheless...someone writes this..it is me.. with pencil and paper here...the author, the writer writes me...the computer doesn't write ...it copies... it is a typewriter, a scribe....i am the machine for writing now... the online material shifts, moves, can be withdrawn ... empty libraries without books... blank screens... no electricity...the book as essential missive... is discounted... they steal it and cut it up... online theft and no property here...the copyright law wobbly, wobbly...anything goes...how to read and what to read now?...i want to read poetry...Baroness Elsa von Freytag-Lovinghoven ...I want to find out more...I want to hold a book now with paper, a spine, the real thing, the essence of writing... but the business model discounts me...the Costco store...giant rolls of toilet paper... we have sales... the bestseller...literature becomes standardised....made palatable, bland...the take away model...few products repeated with few products...means of production now... a factory.... newspapers with big pages without content...advertising... I sell a book here....government policy that doesn't fund culture... we will fund sport but not culture...NO!....people can live without it , says the ambassador... repression, erasure, a flattening... everybody will think the same at the same time...let us repeat now...I love my country...it starts with poetry...the big publisher abandons me...the business model abandons difference, poetry, marginality... we want sales... the literature as a business, a commodity...the airport book... the page turner... don't be too difficult now...speak to everybody... the lowest common denominator... we want simple form, we want a series, tv show and a film and sale of toys and trinkets… the whole shebang, says the accountant…because we lost the book subsidy… because we lost the policy…because we lost culture…the palace of culture now…the syndicated press, the bland voice that says reality television talk…the blah blah blah…I say drivel like James Joyce… at least that…the discounting of intellectual voice… no complex words…keep it simple now… a flattening…the online cruise that says little bits of nothing, sweet nothing…the narrative of the bestseller… the realistic matter fit for purpose now…I will make a tv series out of this…a social commentary….the small publisher now… independently funded press…city lights and black sparrow…that have survived till now… but here…an erosion… a collapse now… a crisis of values… a destruction…they destroy me and burn my book down…Hitler burns books in 1930's…the university , based on the book, reverses and now wants to cut the link… there's cutting and cost cutting … and cutting… a self-mutilation now… an amputation …removing knowledge, richness, variety and plenty…. I cut my finger…… we will give less…we will have less…we will say less and less…I am a robot now… what happened to me?...i cannot speak now…voicelessness… silence…a shutting and shutting down…we are burning the library of Alexandria… we shut a press… a shushing…what will never be done or said…no growth or movement…the creek dries up…who is the critic now…defunded… empty…nothing …in the beginning was the word and now there is

White blankets

White blankets
White blankets
Get your rations,

white flour and your blanket

Infested and distributed

The pillars weave strands
through everyday talk and actions
Alive in the mind

Whiteness descends, pushes, infiltrates
covers and smothers
life rots and dies

Everything, dying

It hides

Ugly things in whiteness
White blankets as god
Slides things through whiteness

Washing through whiteness

Pillars double talk

Intensities move
Weave and tighten
Threads of white meanings

A language of lies
coalesce and crash

Victims alike

Trying to witness,
                    not be drowned
Trying to see
                    Clearly, cleanly

Trying to smell,
                    Sweet air, Sweet air

Pushing through the thick stale veils

Of the blankets of whiteness.

White blanket II

Blankets, blankets, come and get your rations and your blanket

The whiteness is biting hard,
swallowing life into its greedy maw.

Nothing escapes the black and red maw of whiteness.
Red from the blood
Black from the ash, the death.

My brothers and sisters destroyed by whiteness.
The air poisoned, acrid, stale, revolting.

Water going, gone
No water, no life for my brothers and sisters

My brothers the trees, wait, wait, patient, knowing the water will come,
Not knowing of whiteness.

My sister, yonga torn from her country,
her mob, no home, no water, no food
whiteness takes,
No giving.

Wish | LACHLAN BROWN

After Dorothea Mackellar's 'Core of My Heart'

> *16sqm of turf. 1 dwarf lemon.*
> *4 Jasmine seedlings. Ornamental arch.*
> *Year-long subscription to* Better Homes and Gardens
> *magazine. Zoloft 50mg/30 pack.*
> *Quote for grey-blue pebblecrete driveway.*
> *1 backyard pond pump (electric).*
> *2 Happy Meals (one with 6 pack of chicken nuggets, one with chicken wrap)*
> *1 Pad Thai Chicken. 1 Katsu Chicken Bento Box.*

Sunburned colorbond roofs in a newly-named
suburb where helicopter searchlights sweep
backyards after dark. SUVs dream of mountains,
arranged in magazine spreads. You flood
us with love and free trade, recalibrated horizons,
scalable images of coastal areas, brochures
about why you will never be settled in Australia.
Land gets released for working families

beyond the ring roads of each capital city,
springloading commuting times. The moon
gleams brightly here through our particulate matter,
ten thousand air conditioning units murmur
alongside each stifling evening. We all long for
the nursery section at Bunnings, dispensing its spray
like incense in the cool of the evening, the rows
of easy-care ferns, the monopoly of ground cover.

Hardcore economists track the country's spending,
as a blank spring sky awaits love and this quarter's
GDP results. Interest rates will remain on hold,
beef prices will rise steadily, and some guy will stuff up
his order before the Red Rooster crows three
times. He'll complain and get his next meal free:
the glistening chicken, the seasoned chips, the
endless loop of soft drink flavours and sizes.

So yeah corporate responsibility gives us all heart,
lands us back next to food security amid emerging
Asian markets. Be sure to alliterate your insurance
risks before you make each claim, the fine print
reads like an eroded paddock where your display
home is being built. You'll be able to watch
films in the home theatre, e.g. epic disaster movies
that surround sound you with safe catastrophes.

You know our hearts are all floor-planned
and self-sacramental, aching to purchase what
we can't afford or ever hope to pay off. These
attempts at understanding negatively gear us,
until we are painted in the shades of every unfinished
renovation idea. Death remembers its equity in bodies,
then after a while it cul-de-sacs us entirely, a curved
smile running through these streets, drawing us home.

Women's Day | *HANI ABDILE*

On International Women's Day
I sat and watched
Powerful women
Sharing, shining their stories
Racing towards the stars

I saw eyes had witnessed
Pain
But turned it into joy.

Saw unity for equality
I was overwhelmed
Empowered
To stand still
To write my fear
To embrace my tear
Each drop is a word.

Then I reflected my own asylum woman
The woman within me
She is walking on a thin thread.
Sharper than razor blade.

She is physically free
Psychologically chained

Her daily life is like milking a cow on sand.

She is an asylum woman.

She has a vision.
But her eyes are blurred.
Bleeding for a stable
Life.

She grew up before her time
With fire burning her tongue
Her feet collapsing.
She is a broken glass
Dropped between continents!
She lives in hope
Determination is painted
In her cells
The asylum woman
Never knows when the day will come
All she has built
Will be taken by an angry
Flood
A system that is designed
To wipe her meaning away

You agree I am a refugee
But keep me in uncertainty
Temporary
Not quite free
To see
What I could be
With a future sure before me

This poem is a note to my unborn child.
You will be born into progress
You will get to know being strong
Is the uniform of every woman

You will read over these notes
You will realize your mama
When she joined the farm
There were already seeds on the ground.
She just gave them water everyday.

But your ayeyo (your grandma) grew up
When roads of equality
Were unknown
When oppression was their only choice

Don't leave your dreams incomplete
Don't leave your mind complicated

Don't let anyone silence your voice.

Wrongs of Woman (after Mary Wollstonecraft) | KATE LILLEY

Sentiments blotted out

> *A blank space about ten characters in length*

wormed [the whole of]

> *note the omission of any*
> *allusion to that circumstance*

embedded account: adversity, propensity
skirts the metropolis

One of the—passing heard my tale
sequel of a dismal story
> *back to my hole*

Accidental converse
brutes I met
> *do not start—dismission—*

She sent him the memoirs written for—
remarks necessary to elucidate
my project of usefulness

Dead heart of a libertine
squalid object

> *an episode seems to have been intended*
> *never committed to paper*

Bastilled—if women have a country—
no debts of mine [fair Roxana]

I forgot to mention—
****
****
****
> *unruffled lake*

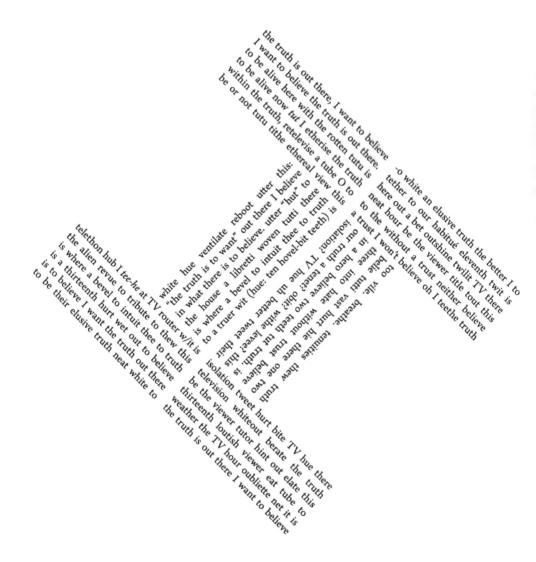

π.O. is a 'famous poet'. After 41 years as a draughtsman he is now retired. He grew up in Fitzroy, and now lives in Darebin. He has published many books the latest being *Big Numbers—New & selected poems, Fitzroy—the Biography,* and *Heide* (which won the Judith Wright Calanthe Award in 2020, and was shortlisted for the Prime Minister's Literary Award for Poetry in the same year). He currently edits the poetry magazine *Unusual Work*, was a founding member of the Poets Union, and performance poetry in Australia. He has also edited an anthology of performance poetry *Off The Record* (1985) with Penguin Books, and *Missing Forms*, an anthology of visual poetry. Has represented Australia, in America, Colombia, Germany, and Thailand.

Hani Abdile is a writer, student and spoken word poet based on Gadigal land, in Sydney. Hani was forced to leave her home country of Somalia and came to Australia seeking protection in 2014. During her 11 months in immigration detention, she found healing in poetry and developed a love for writing. Her first book of poems, *I will rise*, was published by Writing Through Fences in 2016. Hani is an honorary member of PEN International, a lead member of Writing Through Fences, and an Ambassador for the Refugee Advice and Casework Service (RACS).

Munira Tabassum Ahmed is a 16-year-old writer. She has produced work for the *Australian Poetry Journal, SOFTBLOW,* Emerging Writers' Festival, *Runway Journal, The Lifted Brow, Cordite,* and elsewhere. She was a 2020–21 curator and moderator for the Sydney Writers' Festival and currently edits *Hyades Magazine*. Recently, she co-hosted a Culture Makers Lab workshop with the Immigration Museum.

Claire Albrecht is a poet, editor and curator from Newcastle NSW. She was the 2019 Emerging Writers Festival fellow at the State Library of Victoria, a 2020 Varuna 'Writing Fire, Writing Drought' fellow, and the 2021 West Darling Arts Writer in Residence. She will (COVID willing) be a resident at the Helene Wurlitzer Foundation, New Mexico in 2022. Claire's debut chapbook *pinky swear* was published in 2018, and her forthcoming manuscript *handshake* was shortlisted for the Puncher & Wattmann First Poetry Book Prize. She is the Guest Poetry Curator for the Newcastle Writers Festival 2021, and Editor-in-Chief of *The Suburban Review*.

Theresa Alice is a senior Eastern Arrernte woman and traditional owner for country east of Mpartnwe Alice Springs. She has strong ties to the Santa Theresa community and lives at Amoonguna, a small community close to Emily Gap, an important dreaming site for the Yeperenye dreaming. Theresa has a long history of working in the Education system and is a passionate advocate of two-ways learning which incorporates First Nations languages in classroom teaching. She has a Masters degree in Indigenous Knowledges from Charles Darwin University and now works at Akeyulerre Healing Centre where she supports traditional healers to pass on their knowledge and experience to younger family members so that the Arrernte healing traditions may be carried on. Her poem 'Metal Bird' is about a big plane that came from USA to Mparntwe Alice Springs. It had a dot painting all over it but the lady who painted it had passed away. Theresa was sleeping in her room at Amoonguna not far from the airport when the plane came in to land. She felt the earth move and thought the sky was cracking with the big sound it made—she says it was as if the land was grieving but happy that the plane was bringing the spirit of that old lady back home.

Eunice Andrada is a Filipina poet, educator, and organizer. Her debut poetry collection *Flood Damages* (Giramondo Publishing, 2018) won the Anne Elder Award and was shortlisted for the Victorian Premier's Literary Award for Poetry and the Mary Gilmore Award. Her second poetry collection *TAKE CARE* (Giramondo Publishing 2021) is out now. Find out more at euniceandrada.com

Chris Andrews, who taught at the Universities of Melbourne and Western Sydney, has published two collections of poems—*Cut Lunch* (Indigo, 2002) and *Lime Green Chair* (Waywiser, 2012)—and translated books of prose fiction, including Roberto Bolaño's *Distant Star* (Harvill, 2003), Selva Almada's *The Wind that Lays Waste* (Graywolf, 2019), and Kaouther Adimi's *Our Riches* (New Directions, 2020).

Manisha Anjali is a writer and artist. She was born in Suva, Fiji, and has lived on Wurundjeri country, Bundjalung country and Tāmaki Makaurau, Aotearoa. Manisha is the founder of *Community Dream Project*, a research and documentation platform for dreams, visions and hallucinations.

Evelyn Araluen is a poet, researcher and co-editor of *Overland Literary Journal* and the author of *Dropbear* (UQP 2021). Her widely published criticism, fiction and poetry has been awarded the Nakata Brophy Prize for Young Indigenous Writers, the Judith Wright Poetry Prize, a Wheeler Centre Next Chapter Fellowship, and a Neilma Sidney Literary Travel Fund grant. Born and raised on Dharug country, she is a descendant of the Bundjalung Nation.

Mona Zahra Attamimi is Arab-Indonesian and lives on the unceded land of the Bediagal people. She lived as a child in Jakarta, Washington DC and Manila, before moving to Australia at age nine. Her poems have been published in various journals and anthologised in the *Contemporary Asian Australian Poets Anthology* and *To Gather Your Leaving: Asian Diaspora Poetry*. She was the recipient of the Asialink Arts 2019 Emerging Writing Residency, in Bandung, Indonesia.

Luke Beesley is a writer, artist and singer-songwriter. In addition to his books, which include the Giramondo-published trilogy *Aqua Spinach* (2018), *Jam Sticky Vision* (2015) and *New Works on Paper* (2013), his poetry has been published widely in Australia and internationally and translated into several languages. He lives in Melbourne. lukebeesley.com

Judith Beveridge is the author of seven volumes of poetry, most recently *Sun Music: New and Selected Poems*, Giramondo Publishing, 2018. She has won many prizes for her poetry including the Philip Hodgins Memorial Medal and the Christopher Brennan Award. She was a co-editor of *Contemporary Australian Poetry* published in 2016. Her work has been studied in schools and universities and has been translated into several languages. She was the poetry editor of *Meanjin* 2005–2016.

Tony Birch is a founding member of the Melbourne School of Discontent. He has published three novels; *The White Girl*, *Ghost River* and *Blood*. He is also the author of *Shadowboxing* and three short story collections, *Father's Day*, *The*

Promise and *Common People*. In 2017 he was awarded the Patrick White Literary Award for his contribution to Australian literature. In 2021 he released two new books, a poetry book, *Whisper Songs* and a new short story collection, *Dark As Last Night*. His website is: tony-birch.com

Peter Boyle is a Sydney-based poet and translator of poetry. He has nine books of poetry published and eight books as a translator of poetry. His most recent collection is *Notes Towards the Dreambook of Endings* (Vagabond Press, 2021). In 2020 his book *Enfolded in the Wings of a Great Darkness* won the New South Wales Premier's Award for Poetry. His translations include four books by Cuban poet José Kozer and *The Trees: Selected Poems of Eugenio Montejo*.

David Brooks' most recent collection is *Open House* (UQP, 2016). Another is in preparation. His latest publications are *Animal Dreams* (essays on the animal in contemporary literature, philosophy and public policy: Sydney University Press, 2021) and *Turin* (meditations: Brandl & Schlesinger, 2021). He taught Australian Literature at the University of Sydney for many years and was co-editor of *Southerly* for almost twenty. He lives in the Blue Mountains with rescued sheep.

Lachlan Brown is a senior lecturer in English at Charles Sturt University, Wagga Wagga. He is the author of *Limited Cities* (Giramondo, 2012) and *Lunar Inheritance* (Giramondo, 2017). Lachlan's poetry has been published in various journals including *Antipodes*, *Cordite*, and *Rabbit*. He has previously been involved in judging the Gwen Harwood Poetry Prize and the Mary Gilmore Poetry Prize.

Pam Brown has been writing, collaborating, editing and publishing in diverse modes for five decades. A number of her many books have been on the shortlists and have sometimes won the prize. In 2019 *Click here* for *what we do* (Vagabond Press) was awarded the ALS Gold Medal. Her new collection, *Stasis Shuffle*, is due soon from Hunter Publishers. Born in Seymour Victoria, Pam grew up on military bases in Toowoomba and Brisbane. She has lived in Melbourne and Adelaide but has spent most of her life in Sydney where, currently, she lives on never-ceded Gadigal land.

joanne burns is a Sydney poet. Her most recent book is *apparently*, Giramondo Publishing 2019. These days she writes in the interstices.

Michelle Cahill was born in Kenya and lives on unceded Guringai lands. They have received prizes in poetry and fiction notably the UTS Glenda Adams Award for *Letter to Pessoa*, the KWS Hilary Mantel International Short Story Competition, the Val Vallis Award and the Red Room Poetry Fellowship. *Vishvarupa* was shortlisted in the Victorian Premier's Literary Awards. *The Herring Lass* was published by Arc. *Woolf* is forthcoming with Hachette.

Derek Chan is a Melbourne-based writer who holds a First-Class Honours in Literary Studies from Monash University. His poems have appeared in both domestic and international journals such as *Meanjin*, *Cordite Poetry Review*, *Voiceworks*, *Verge* and *Juked*.

Eileen Chong is a Sydney poet. She is the author of nine books. Her work has been shortlisted for many prizes, including the NSW Premier's Literary Awards, the Victorian Premier's Literary Awards, and twice for the Prime Minister's Literary Awards. Her most recent poetry collection is *A Thousand Crimson Blooms* from the University of Queensland Press. She lives and works on unceded Gadigal land of the Eora Nation. eileenchong.com.au

Aidan Coleman has published three collections of poetry, most recently *Mount Sumptuous* (Wakefield Press, 2020). He is currently completing *Thin Ice: A Life of John Forbes* that will be published by Melbourne University Publishing. Aidan is an Early Career Researcher at the J.M. Coetzee Centre for Creative Practice at the University of Adelaide.

Rico Craig is an educator, writer, and award-winning poet whose work melds the narrative, lyrical and cinematic. Craig is published widely; his poetry has been awarded prizes or shortlisted for the Montreal Poetry Prize, Val Vallis Prize, Newcastle Poetry Prize, Dorothy Porter Poetry Prize and University of Canberra Poetry Prize. His poetry collection *Bone Ink* (University of Western Australia Publishing) was winner of the 2017 Anne Elder Award and shortlisted for the Kenneth Slessor Poetry Prize 2018. *Our Tongues Are Songs*, his second collection of poetry, was published in 2021 by Recent Work Press.

Louise Crisp is the author of *Yuiquimbiang* (Cordite Books) shortlisted for the Victorian Premier's Literary Awards 2020. Her latest collection is *Glide* (Puncher & Wattmann, 2021). An e-chapbook *Coupe Portraits: walking the damaged forests of East Gippsland (Gunaikurnai country)* was published by Cordite Poetry Review in May 2021. Her writing focuses on specific regional environments of south-eastern Australia and experiments with the formal possibilities of integrating poetics and environmental activism.

Judith Nangala Crispin is an artist and poet. She's published two volumes of poetry, *The Myrrh-Bearers* (Puncher & Wattmann) and *The Lumen Seed* (Daylight Books), and has a third on the way. In an earlier incarnation Judith published a scholarly book on music that nobody will ever read. She also rides motorcycles and spends months of each year in the desert with her dingo 'Moon' and Warlpiri friends.

Josie/Jocelyn Deane is a programmer/freelance writer/editor at the University of Melbourne. Their work has appeared in *The Suburban Review, Rabbit Journal, Australian Poetry Journal* and *Overland*, among others. They have featured in the 2020 Melbourne Spoken Word and Poetry Festival, and in 2021 they were one of the recipients of the Queensland Poetry Festival Ekphrasis award, as well as the 2021 Ultimo Press Poetry Prize. They are a genderqueer transfemme. They live on unceded Wurundjeri land.

Shastra Deo was born in Fiji, raised in Melbourne, and lives in Brisbane. Her first book, *The Agonist* (UQP 2017), won the 2016 Arts Queensland Thomas Shapcott Poetry Prize and the 2018 Australian Literature Society Gold Medal. Her second book, *The Exclusion Zone*, is forthcoming from University of Queensland Press in 2023.

Dave Drayton was an amateur banjo player, founding member of the Atterton Academy, and the author of *E, UIO, A: a feghoot* (Container), *A pet per ably-faced kid* (Stale Objects dePress), *P(oe)Ms* (Rabbit), *Haiturograms* (Stale Objects dePress) and *Poetic Pentagons* (Spacecraft Press).

Jonathan Dunk is the co-editor of *Overland*, and a widely published writer. He has received the AD Hope prize and the Dal Stivens award; lectures at Deakin University, and lives on Wurundjeri country.

Ali Cobby Eckermann's first collection *little bit long time* was written in the desert and launched her literary career in 2009. In 2013 Ali toured Ireland as Australian Poetry Ambassador and won the Kenneth Slessor Prize for Poetry and Book Of The Year (NSW) for *Ruby Moonlight*, a massacre verse novel. In 2014 Ali was the inaugural recipient of the Tungkunungka Pintyanthi Fellowship at Adelaide Writers Week for her memoir *Too Afraid To Cry*, and the first Aboriginal Australian writer to attend the International Writing Program at University of Iowa. In 2017 Ali received a Windham Campbell Award for Poetry from Yale University USA and was awarded a Literature Fellowship by the Australian Council for the Arts in 2018. Ali is currently an Adjunct Professor at RMIT Melbourne and is employed as Arts & Cultural Facilitator for Goyder Council in Burra SA.

Huda Fadlelmawla is a young African poet who has been given the responsibility by her ancestors of using her voice to share stories and have conversations with people's souls. She believes that art has the ability to heal nations by allowing our emotions and thoughts to be let out in the most beautiful way.

Michael Farrell has published several books of poetry, including, most recently, *Family Trees* (2020), and *I Love Poetry* (2017), which won the Judith Wright Calanthe Queensland Award for Poetry (both published by Giramondo). Michael has a scholarly book, *Writing Australian Unsettlement: Modes of Poetic Invention 1796–1945* (Palgrave Macmillan), and has also edited two anthologies, *Ashbery Mode* (Tin Fish, 2019), and *Out of the Box: Contemporary Gay and Lesbian Australian Poets* (Puncher and Wattmann, 2009). Michael's artwork (collage, ceramics, drawing and painting) can be seen on instagram: @limechax.

Liam Ferney's most recent collection *Hot Take* (Hunter Publishing) was shortlisted for the Judith Wright Calanthe Award. His previous volumes include *Content* (Hunter Publishing) and *Boom* (Grande Parade Poets). He is a public affairs manager, poet and aspiring left-back living in Brisbane with his wife and daughter.

Zenobia Frost is an arts writer and award-winning poet based in Brisbane, Australia. Her most recent poetry collection, *After the Demolition* (Cordite Books), won the 2020 Wesley Michel Wright Award and was shortlisted for the NSW Premier's Literary Awards. She recently received a Queensland Premier's Young Publishers and Writers Award and, in 2020, edited coffee-table history book *Art Starts Here: 40 Years of Metro Arts*.

Lou Garcia-Dolnik is a poet and editor working on unceded Gadigal land. Their writing has been awarded second prize in *Overland*'s Judith Wright Poetry Prize, a place on the shortlist for the 2020 Blake and 2021 Val Vallis Awards, and an Academy of American Poets University Prize from the University of Texas at Austin in 2021. A poetry editor for *Voiceworks* and alumnus of the Banff Centre's Emerging Writers Intensive, they are a 2020–21 Wheeler Centre Hot Desk Fellow and Varuna Residential Fellow.

Juan Garrido-Salgado immigrated to Australia from Chile in 1990, fleeing the regime that burned his poetry and imprisoned and tortured him for his political activism. He has published eight books of poetry and his work has been widely translated. He has also translated works by a number of leading Australian and Aboriginal poets into Spanish, including five Aboriginal poets for the anthology *Espejo de Tierra/ Earth Mirror* (2008). With Steve Brock and Sergio Holas, Garrido-Salgado also translated into English the Trilingual Mapuche Poetry Anthology. The book *When I was Clandestine* was part of a poetical tour at the Granada International Poetry Festival in Nicaragua, Mexico and Cuba (La Habana City) in 2019. He published *Hope Blossoming in Their Ink* (Puncher & Wattmann) in 2020. Three of his poems were published at saturdaypaper.com May '21.

Jake Goetz has published one book, *meditations with passing water* (Rabbit Poets Series), which was shortlisted for the QLD Premier's Award in 2019. He is currently undertaking a DCA at the Writing & Society Research Centre (WSU).

Elena Gomez is the author of *Admit the Joyous Passion of Revolt*, *Body of Work* and several chapbooks and pamphlets.

Lisa Gorton writes poetry, fiction and essays. Her two most recent publications, both from Giramondo, are the novel *The Life of Houses* and her poetry collection, *Empirical*. Lisa also recently contributed a sequence of poems to Izabela Pluta's artist's book *Figures of Slippage and Oscillation* (Perimeter Press). 'Mirabilia' is the title poem of Lisa's forthcoming poetry collection.

Charmaine Papertalk Green is an award-winning poet from Midwest Western Australia and a member of the Wajarri, Badimaya and Nhanagardi Wilunyu cultural groups of the Yamaji Nation. Her publications include *Just Like That* (Fremantle Art Press, 2007); *Tiptoeing Tod the Tracker* (Oxford University Press, 2014); collaboration with WA poet John Kinsella, *False Claim of Colonial Thieves* (Magabala Books, 2018); *Nganajungu Yagu* (Cordite Publishing Inc.'s, 2019); and numerous anthologies and other publications. She lives in Geraldton WA.

Joy Harjo is an internationally renowned performer and writer of the Muscogee (Creek) Nation. She is serving her third term as the 23rd Poet Laureate of the United States. The author of nine books of poetry, including the highly acclaimed *An American Sunrise*, several plays and children's books, and two memoirs, *Crazy Brave* and *Poet Warrior*, her many honors include the Ruth Lily Prize for Lifetime Achievement from the Poetry Foundation, the Academy of American Poets Wallace Stevens Award, two NEA fellowships, and a Guggenheim Fellowship. As a musician and performer, Harjo has produced seven award-winning music albums including her newest, *I Pray for My Enemies*. She is Executive Editor of the anthology *When the Light of the World was Subdued, Our Songs Came Through—A Norton Anthology of Native Nations Poetry* and the editor of *Living Nations, Living Words: An Anthology of First Peoples Poetry*, the companion anthology to her signature Poet Laureate project. She is a chancellor of the Academy of American Poets, Board of Directors Chair of the Native Arts & Cultures Foundation, and holds a Tulsa Artist Fellowship. She lives in Tulsa, Oklahoma.

Natalie Harkin is a Narungga woman and activist-poet from South Australia. She is a Senior Research Fellow at Flinders University with an interest in decolonising state archives, currently engaging archival-poetic methods to research and document Aboriginal women's domestic service and labour histories in SA. Her words have been installed and projected in exhibitions comprising text-object-video projection, including creative-arts research collaboration with the *Unbound Collective*. She has published widely, and her poetry manuscripts include *Dirty Words* with Cordite Books in 2015, and *Archival-poetics* with Vagabond Press in 2019.

Lujayn Hourani is a Lebanese-Palestinian writer, editor, and arts worker living on unceded Wurundjeri Country. They are a 2020 recipient of the Wheeler Centre's Next Chapter scheme and are currently working on a book of experimental poetry about suffocation and the Israeli occupation of Palestine. Their work has previously been published in *Meanjin*, *Overland*, and *Going Down Swinging*, among others.

Noémie Cecilia Huttner-Koros is a queer Jewish performance-maker, writer, teaching artist, dramaturg and community organiser living on Whadjuk Noongar country, who grew up on Ngunnuwal country in Canberra. Noémie's practice engages with sites and histories where ecological crisis, queer culture and composting occur. Her work has taken place in theatres, galleries, alleyways, dinner parties and blanket forts. Her poetry has been featured in *Australian Poetry Anthology 2020*, *Rabbit Poetry Journal*, Perth Poetry Festival and she was the winner of the 2020 Venie Holmgren Environmental Poetry Prize.

Andy Jackson has been shortlisted for the Kenneth Slessor Prize for Poetry and the John Bray Poetry Award, and has co-edited disability-themed issues of *Southerly* and *Australian Poetry Journal*. In 2019, his PhD thesis, *Disabling Poetics: Bodily Otherness and the Saying of Poetry*, was awarded a Doctoral Research Medal for Outstanding Academic Achievement by the University of Adelaide. He works as a creative writing teacher and tutor for community organisations and universities, and his latest poetry collection is *Human Looking* (Giramondo, 2021).

Ella Jeffery is a poet and editor. Her debut collection of poems, *Dead Bolt*, won the Puncher & Wattmann Prize for a First Book of Poems and the Anne Elder Award, and was shortlisted for the Mary Gilmore Award. She is a recipient of the Queensland Premier's Young Publishers and Writers Award, a Queensland Writers Fellowship, and her poetry has appeared widely in journals and anthologies including *Best Australian Poems*, *Meanjin*, *Griffith Review* and *Southerly*. She lives in Brisbane.

Jill Jones was born in Sydney and has lived in Adelaide since 2008. Recent books include *Wild Curious Air,* winner of the 2021 Wesley Michel Wright Prize, *A History Of What I'll Become,* shortlisted for the 2021 Kenneth Slessor Award, and *Viva the Real,* shortlisted for the 2019 Prime Minister's Literary Award for Poetry and the 2020 John Bray Award. In 2015 she won the Victorian Premier's Prize for Poetry for *The Beautiful Anxiety.* Her work is widely published in Australia and internationally. She has worked as an academic for a number of years, but also as an arts administrator, journalist, and book editor.

John Kinsella's most recent volumes of poetry include *Drowning in Wheat: Selected Poems 1980–2015* (Picador, 2016), *Open Door* (UWAP, 2018), *Insomnia* (WW Norton, 2020) and *Supervivid Depastoralism* (Vagabond, 2021). University of Western Australia Press will be publishing his *Collected Poems 1980–2021* in three volumes, with the first volume being released in early 2022. He is Emeritus Professor at Curtin University, and lives with his family in wheatbelt Western Australia on Ballardong Noongar country.

Yeena Kirkbright is a Wiradjuri poet who grew up in Central West New South Wales, she now lives and works on Wangal, Darug and Gadigal lands. Her work has been published in several literary journals.

Louis Klee's poetry has appeared in the *Times Literary Supplement,* the *Cambridge Literary Review, Cordite, Meanjin, Best Australian Poems,* and the *Australian Book Review.* He won the Peter Porter Prize for his poem 'Sentence to Lilacs'.

Shari Kocher is the author of *Foxstruck and Other Collisions* (Puncher & Wattmann, 2021) and *The Non-Sequitur of Snow* (Puncher & Wattmann, 2015), which was Highly Commended in the 2015 Anne Elder Awards (Australia). Recent awards include The Peter Steele Poetry Prize (2019) and The Venie Holmgren Environmental Poetry Award (2018). She holds MA and Doctorate degrees from Melbourne University, where she sometimes works as a sessional teaching associate in the creative writing program.

Abbra Kotlarczyk is an artist, curator, writer and editor invested in expanded and sensorial modes of reading. She was raised on the unceded lands of the Arakwal peoples and currently lives, works and raises her family on Wurundjeri Woiworung Country in Naarm/Melbourne. *Debris Facility* is a para-corporate entity founded in 2015 to interrupt value exchanges. Institutionally affiliated with Liquid Architecture and VCA, they work 24/7 on stolen land, water, air.

Kristen Lang's *Earth Dwellers* was published in 2021 by Giramondo. She lives in north-west Tasmania and is working on ways to use poetry as part of our cultural response to the Anthropocene. In 2021, with support from AP, Kristen founded the More Than Human Poetry Project, leading to new works from 24 Tasmanian poets. Her *SkinNotes* (Walleah Press) and *The Weight of Light* (Five Islands Press) were published in 2017.

Jeanine Leane is a Wiradjuri writer, essayist, and poet. She is living and working on Wurundjeri Lands at the University of Melbourne where she teaches writing. She is an award-winning poet and her essays have been widely published in literary journals in Australia and abroad.

Bella Li is the author of *Argosy* (Vagabond Press, 2017), *Lost Lake* (Vagabond Press, 2018) and *Theory of Colours* (Vagabond Press, 2021). She holds a PhD from the University of Melbourne and is the associate publisher at Cordite Books.

Kate Lilley (1960–) is a queer, Sydney-based poet and academic. She is the author of 3 books of poetry, most recently *Tilt* (Vagabond 2018), winner of the Victorian Premier's Award for Poetry.

Janiru Liyanage is a 16-year-old school student and poet. He has been nominated for a Pushcart Prize, Best New Poets and Best of the Net with recent work appearing or featured in/on *The Harvard Advocate*, *The Australian*, *DIAGRAM*, *Waxwing*, *[PANK]*, and elsewhere. He was longlisted for The 2020 Frontier Industry Prize, edits for *Hyades Magazine* and has produced work for Australian Poetry, the Wheeler Centre, and the Emerging Writers' Festival, among other places. Born as the son of Sinhalese immigrants, he currently lives in Australia.

Grace Lucas-Pennington is an Aboriginal (Bundjalung) editor specialising in First Nations fiction and poetry. She grew up mostly between northern NSW and the greater Logan/Brisbane area. Grace is the Senior Editor at State Library of Queensland's black&write! Indigenous Writing and Editing Project. She was awarded the 2020 Nakata Brophy prize for poetry.

Kent MacCarter is the author of three poetry collections and is director of Cordite Publishing Inc.

Kate Middleton is the author of *Fire Season* (2009), awarded the Western Australian Premier's Award for Poetry, *Ephemeral Waters* (2013), shortlisted for the NSW Premier's award, and *Passage* (2017).

Peter Minter is a poet, poetry editor and writer on poetry and poetics.

Audrey Molloy grew up in Ireland and lives in Sydney. Her first collection, *The Important Things*, is published by The Gallery Press (2021). She is the author of *Satyress* (Southword Editions, 2020). Her work has appeared in *Meanjin*, *Cordite*, *Overland*, *Australian Poetry Anthology*, *Southerly*, *Rabbit Poetry Journal*, *Red Room Poetry (In Your Hands)*, *The Australian* and *Verity La*. In 2019 she was runner up in the Newcastle Poetry Prize and in 2020 she was awarded a Varuna Residency Fellowship.

Jazz Money is an award-winning poet of Wiradjuri heritage, a fresh water woman currently based on beautiful Gadigal land now known as Sydney. Her practice is centred around the written word while producing works that encompass installation, digital, film and print. Jazz's David Unaipon Award winning debut collection *how to make a basket* is available from University of Queensland Press.

David Musgrave's 8th collection is his *Selected Poems*, published in the UK this year. He teaches creative writing at the University of Newcastle and is the founder of Puncher & Wattmann, of which he is Managing Director.

Jennifer Nguyen is the author of *When I die slingshot my ashes onto the surface of the moon* (Subbed In, 2019). In 2019, Jennifer was awarded a Wheeler Centre Hot Desk Fellowship for poetry.

Damen O'Brien is a multi-award-winning Brisbane poet. His awards include the Moth Poetry Prize, the Newcastle Poetry Prize and the Val Vallis Award. Damen's poems have been published in many journals including *Mississippi Review*, *Atlanta Review*, *Crosswinds* and *Southwords*. Damen's first book of poetry, *Animals With Human Voices,* is available through Recent Work Press. www.dameno.org

Thuy On is Reviews Editor of ArtsHub, She's an arts journalist, critic, editor and poet. Her first collection of poetry, *Turbulence*, was published in 2020 by UWAP.

Kaya Ortiz is an emerging writer and poet from the southern islands of Mindanao and lutruwita/Tasmania. Her writing has appeared in *Portside Review*, *Westerly*, *Tell Me Like You Mean It Vol 4*, and *After Australia*, among others. In 2019, they were a Hot Desk Fellow at the Centre for Stories in Boorloo/Perth and a participant in Express Media/Australian Poetry's Toolkits: Poetry program. Kaya currently lives in Boorloo/Perth, where their name means 'hello' in the Nyoongar language.

Ouyang Yu has published 137 books in both English and Chinese in the field of fiction, nonfiction, poetry, literary translation and criticism. His second book of English poetry, *Songs of the Last Chinese Poet*, was shortlisted for the 1999 NSW Premier's Literary Award. His third novel, *The English Class*, won the 2011 NSW Premier's Award, and his translation in Chinese of *The Fatal Shore* by Robert Hughes won the Translation Award from the Australia-China Council in 2014. He won the Judith Wright Calanthe Award for a Poetry Collection in the 2021 Queensland Literary Awards. His bilingual blog at: youyang2.blogspot.com

Luke Patterson is a Gamilaroi poet, folklorist, musician and educator living on Gadigal lands. He is interested in the ways bioregional identities and consciousness are expressed through localised and vernacular forms. Luke's research and creative pursuits are grounded in his extensive work with Aboriginal and other community-based organisations across Australia.

Anupama Pilbrow writes poems about gross, stinky, delightful things. Her work appears in journals and anthologies including *Cordite Poetry Review*, *Rabbit Poetry Journal*, *JEASA*, *Southerly*, *Liminal*, and *The Hunter Anthology of Contemporary Australian Feminist Poetry*. Read her chapbook *Body Poems*, out with Vagabond Press 2018.

Felicity Plunkett is an award-winning poet and critic. She is the author of *A Kinder Sea* (UQP), *Vanishing Point* (UQP) and the chapbook *Seastrands* (Vagabond), published in Vagabond Press' Rare Objects series. She edited *Thirty Australian Poets* (UQP, 2011). Felicity has a PhD from the University of Sydney and was Poetry Editor with University of Queensland Press for nine years. She is a widely-published reviewer and critic, and a respected mentor of other writers.

Isabel Prior is a junior doctor from Brisbane who wishes she had written *Normal People*. She would be comfortably retired, spending her days reading Seamus Heaney, Sharon Olds and Elizabeth Bishop.

Jinghua Qian is a Shanghainese-Melburnian writer often found worrying about race, resistance, art, desire, queerness and the Chinese diaspora. Ey has been a performance poet, a radio broadcaster, a television journalist, and an arts critic. Eir work has appeared in *The Guardian, The Saturday Paper, Sydney Morning Herald, Overland, Meanjin*, and *Peril*, on ABC TV's China Tonight, and once on a brick wall. Jinghua lives in Melbourne's west on the land of the Kulin Nations.

Daley Rangi is a Māori antidisciplinary artist generating unpredictable works and words. Speaking truth to power and reorienting hierarchies, Daley is inspired by ancestry and fuelled by injustice.

Ursula Robinson-Shaw is a writer from Aotearoa, living on Wurundjeri land.

Gig Ryan's *New and Selected Poems* (Giramondo, 2011; *Selected Poems*, Bloodaxe Books, U.K.), was winner of the 2012 Grace Leven Prize for Poetry and the 2012 Kenneth Slessor Prize for Poetry. She has also written songs with Disband, Six Goodbyes (1988), and Driving Past, Real Estate (1999), Travel (2006). She was Poetry Editor of *The Age* from 1998–2016. She is a freelance reviewer; next book forthcoming 2022.

Omar Sakr is the author of *These Wild Houses* (Cordite, 2017) and *The Lost Arabs* (UQP, 2019), which won the 2020 Prime Minister's Literary Award for Poetry. His poems have been published and anthologised in places such as the Academy of American Poets Poem-a-Day series, *Border Lines: Poems of Migration* (Vintage Knopf, 2020), the *Anthology of Australian Prose Poetry* (MUP, 2020) *Best Australian Poems* (Black Inc, 2016) and *Contemporary Australian Poetry* (Puncher & Wattmann, 2016). Born and raised on Dharug country to Lebanese and Turkish Muslim migrants, he lives there still. His debut novel, *Son of Sin*, is forthcoming with Affirm Press.

Sara M Saleh is a human rights activist and the daughter of migrants from Palestine, Egypt, and Lebanon, living on Gadigal land. A poet and writer, her pieces have been published in English and Arabic in various national and international outlets and anthologies including *Australian Poetry Journal, Cordite Poetry Review, Meanjin, Overland* and *Rabbit* Poetry. She is co-editor of the 2019 anthology *Arab, Australian, Other: Stories on Race and Identity*. Sara is the first poet to win both the *Australian Book Review's* 2021 Peter Porter Poetry Prize and the *Overland* Judith Wright Poetry Prize 2020. She is currently developing her first novel as a recipient of the inaugural Affirm Press Mentorship for Sweatshop Western Sydney.

Mykaela Saunders is a Koori and Lebanese writer, teacher, community researcher, and the editor of *THIS ALL COME BACK NOW*, the world's first anthology of blackfella speculative fiction, forthcoming with UQP in 2022. Mykaela has won the Elizabeth Jolley Short Story Prize, the National Indigenous Story Award, the

Oodgeroo Noonuccal Indigenous Poetry Prize, the Grace Marion Wilson Emerging Writers Prize and the University of Sydney's Sister Alison Bush Graduate Medal. Of Dharug descent, and working-class and queer, Mykaela belongs to the Tweed Goori community. mykaelasaunders.com

Jaya Savige is an Australian poet and editor currently based in London. His most recent poetry collection is *Change Machine* (UQP 2020). His previous collections include *Latecomers* (UQP), which won the NSW Premier's Kenneth Slessor Prize for Poetry, and *Surface to Air* (UQP), which was shortlisted for *The Age* Poetry Book of the Year and the West Australian Premier's Prize. A former Gates Scholar at the University of Cambridge, he is poetry editor for the Weekend Australian, and has held Australia Council residencies at the B.R. Whiting Library, Rome, and the Cité Internationale des Arts, Paris.

Brooke Scobie is a queer Goorie woman, single mum, poetry and prose writer, podcast host and community worker. Born and bred on Bidjigal country, and now living on Darkinjung land, she considers herself first and foremost a creative weirdo. As a writer she is dedicated to telling stories that centre Blak identities, queer love, family, and unpacking some of the issues that can affect First Nations' communities and countries. Brooke has been published in *Overland, Running Dog*, Red Room Poetry, SBS and was awarded second place in the 2020 Judith Wright Poetry Prize.

Melinda Smith is a poet, editor, teacher and performer. Her latest book is *Man-handled* (Recent Work Press, 2020). She is the author of seven other poetry books, including the 2014 Prime Minister's Literary Award winner, *Drag down to unlock or place an emergency call*, and her work has been widely anthologised and translated. Recently she co-edited the *Australian Poetry Anthology Vol. 8* with Sara M Saleh, and *Borderless: A Transnational Anthology of Feminist Poetry* with Saba Vasefi and Yvette Holt. She is a former poetry editor of *The Canberra Times*, and lives and writes on unceded Ngunnawal Country.

Snack Syndicate (Astrid Lorange and Andrew Brooks) is a critical art collective who live and work on Wangal country. They make texts, objects, meals, and events. *Homework*, a book of essays and poems, was published by Discipline in 2021. They both lecture at UNSW and are members of the Infrastructural Inequalities research network and the Rosa Press publishing collective.

Danny Silva Soberano is a poet.

David Stavanger is a poet, performer, cultural producer, editor and former psychologist living on unceded Dharawal land. His first full-length poetry collection *The Special* (UQP, 2014) was awarded the Arts Queensland Thomas Shapcott Poetry Prize and the Wesley Michel Wright Poetry Prize. He is the co-editor of *Australian Poetry Journal* 8.2—'spoken', *Rabbit* 27 Tense and *SOLID AIR: Collected Australian & New Zealand Spoken Word* (UQP, 2019.) His latest collection *Case Notes* (UWAP, 2020) won the 2021 Victorian Premier's Literary Award for Poetry.

Emily Stewart lives and works on Wangal land. She is a freelance writer and editor and is currently completing a doctorate at the Writing and Society Research Centre. She is the author of *Knocks* (Vagabond Press, 2016) and numerous chapbooks including *The Internet Blue* (Firstdraft 2017).

Andrew Sutherland (he/him) is a Queer Poz (PLHIV) writer and performance-maker between Boorloo and Singapore. He was awarded *Overland's* Fair Australia Poetry Prize 2017 and placed third in FAWWA's Tom Collins Prize 2021. His poetry, fiction and non-fiction can be found in numerous journals and anthologies, including *Westerly, Cordite, Portside Review, Running Dog,* 聲韻詩刊 *Voice & Verse, EXHALE: an Anthology of Queer voices from Singapore* (Math Paper Press), and Margaret River Press' *We'll Stand in That Place*. His debut collection is forthcoming with Fremantle Press in 2022. He is grateful to reside on Whadjuk Noongar land.

Dominic Symes lives and writes in Naarm (Melbourne). His poetry has appeared in *Overland, Cordite, Australian Book Review,* and *Australian Poetry Journal*. He curates NO WAVE, a monthly poetry reading series on Kaurna Country (Adelaide) where he grew up and which he gets nostalgic about sometimes. He was selected for *Cordite/AP's Tell me like you mean it* 4 anthology and appeared at the Emerging Writers' Festival in 2020. He is yet to publish a book of poems but would like to.

Heather Taylor-Johnson lives and writes on Kaurna land near Port Adelaide. Her last novel was *Jean Harley was Here*, recently optioned for a tv series, and she is the editor of *Shaping the Fractured Self: Poetry of Chronic Illness and Pain*. Her fifth book of poetry is a hybrid epistolary verse novel called *Rhymes with Hyenas*. A new collection—*Alternative Hollywood Ending*—is due out in 2022.

Sarah Temporal is a poet, writer, mother, events host and educator from the Northern Rivers NSW. Her work has been twice shortlisted for the Arts Queensland XYZ Prize for Innovation in Spoken Word. Her poetry appears in the *Australian Poetry Anthology, Cordite, Women of Words* anthology, *Not-Very-Quiet*, and other Australian literary journals. She runs Poets Out Loud, a regional initiative for writing and spoken-word, and looks forward to releasing her debut poetry collection.

Werte, my name is *Shirley Kngwarraye Turner*. I am from Anapipe, Sandybore Outstation which it's about 85km northeast of Mparntwe, Alice Springs. I am central Arrernte woman and a mother of four children and three grannies. I come from strong families who respect countries and culture. I am youngest in my family, I've got six siblings who all have families of their own. We all grew up knowing McGraths Dam, a special place where we used to go out and stay with our parents and grandparents when they were taking us back to country. I wrote this poem because Althateme, McGraths Dam is our apmere, the place we all call home. Its important to all our families, and to the history of Land Rights. I also wrote it because I really enjoy poetry and other creative writing.

Lucy Van writes poetry and criticism. She has been a writer in residence at *Overland* (2019–2020), and a Melbourne Research Fellow at the University of Melbourne

(2018–2019). Her forthcoming publications include a long-form essay about Australia, southeast Asia and the possibilities of decolonial travel, and a monograph called *The Beginning of the Poem*. Her first poetry collection is *The Open* (Cordite Books, 2021).

Dženana Vucic is a Bosnian-Australian writer, poet and critic. She has received the 2021 Kat Muscat Fellowship and a 2020–21 Wheeler Centre Hot Desk Fellowship to work on an autotheoretical book about her experience as a refugee, the Bosnian war, identity, memory and un/belonging. Her writing has appeared in *Cordite, Overland, Meanjin, Kill Your Darlings, Australian Poetry Journal*, the *Australian Multilingual Writing Project, Rabbit*, and others. She tweets at @dzenanabanana.

Tais Rose Wae is a writer and weaver living on sovereign Bundjalung Country. With a complex displaced cultural identification developed through the ongoing process of colonisation, her poetry celebrates the inevitable strength and resilience of her Aboriginal ancestry. She was the 2020 runner-up for the Nakata Brophy Prize for Young Indigenous Writers, was highly commended for the Wheeler Centre's The Next Chapter in 2020 and was shortlisted for the Oodgeroo Noonuccal Indigenous Poetry Prize in 2021. Her work has been published in the *Australian Poetry Anthology, Overland Literary Journal, Westerly, Running Dog, Knus Magazine* and *Paradiso*.

Aileen Marwung Walsh is fortunate to have a unique perspective of the past, the climate disaster and culture and society generally having undergraduate degrees in the social sciences as well as currently working in the discipline of history for her doctoral research project which examines the past for how climate change and mass extinctions happened. Her research uses neurobiology to underpin her argument on how to care for country. Aileen grew up learning Aboriginal ways of knowing which means an uncivilised outlook. This was in stark contrast to what she learned as a Bahai and the role of religions in the past and the present.

Dr Ania Walwicz (1951–2020) was an avant-garde poet, author, playwright, performer, and artist. She was a distinguished teacher at RMIT University, and writer-in-residence at various Australian universities. Ania was a graduate of Victorian College of the Arts, University of Melbourne, and Deakin University. Her fictocritical book *Horse: A Psychodramatic Enactment of a Fairy Tale* won the Alfred Deakin Medal, 2017. Her work has been published in several collections, included in over 200 anthologies, and performed for theatre, opera and spoken-word locally and internationally. Ania emigrated from Świdnica, Poland to Melbourne, Australia in 1963 when she was 12 years old.

Petra White lives in Berlin. Her latest collection is *Cities* (Vagabond Press 2021).

Alison Whittaker is a Gomeroi poet and academic. She is Senior Researcher at the Jumbunna Institute.

Jessica L. Wilkinson has published three poetic biographies, most recently *Music Made Visible: A Biography of George Balanchine* (Vagabond Press, 2019). She is the founding editor of *Rabbit: a journal for nonfiction poetry* and the offshoot Rabbit Poets Series. She is an associate professor in creative writing at RMIT University.

Grace Yee is a poet, writer and researcher based in Melbourne. Her work has appeared in *Overland, Meanjin, Southerly, Westerly, The Shanghai Literary Review, Women's Museum of California, Hecate, Hainamana*, and *Poetry New Zealand Yearbook*, among others. In 2020, Grace was awarded the Patricia Hackett Prize, and the Peter Steele Poetry Award. From 2019 to 2021 she was a Creative Fellow at the State Library Victoria, where she worked on a collection of poems engaging with the histories of early Chinese settlers in Melbourne and regional Victoria. A chapbook from this collection, *A Special Starch*, was published by *Cordite Poetry Review* in 2021. www.graceyeepoet.com

Guest Editor Biographies

Ellen van Neerven is an award-winning writer of Mununjali and Dutch heritage. Their books include *Heat and Light*, *Comfort Food* and *Throat*. ellenvanneervencurrie.wordpress.com

Toby Fitch is poetry editor of *Overland*, a lecturer in creative writing at the University of Sydney, and the director of AVANT GAGA and the Poetry Night at Sappho Books. He is the author of seven books of poetry, including *Where Only the Sky had Hung Before* and, most recently, *Sydney Spleen*. tobyfitch.net

Acknowledgements and Publication Details

π.O.'s 'Exact/Inexact' appeared in *Meanjin*, Winter 2021.

Hani Abdile's 'Women's Day' was performed on *Q+A*, March 2021.

Munira Tabassum Ahmed's 'Glossary for Our Women' appeared in *Cordite Poetry Review*, February 2021.

Claire Albrecht's 'creation lament' appeared in *Minarets* 11, August 2020.

Theresa Penangke Alice's 'Metal bird' appeared in *Arelhekenhe Angkentye: Women's Talk: Poems of Lyapirtneme from Arrernte Women in Central Australia*, Running Water Community Press, August 2020.

Eunice Andrada's 'Nature is Healing' was performed on the podcast *Extraordinary Voices For Extraordinary Times*, episode 1, July 2020, and then appeared in her collection *TAKE CARE*, Giramondo Publishing, 2021.

Chris Andrews' 'Suite of Powers' appeared in *Island* 162, July 2021.'

Manisha Anjali's 'NAUSEA' appeared in *Liminal*, October 2020.

Evelyn Araluen's 'Breath' appeared in her collection *Dropbear*, University of Queensland Press, March 2021.

Mona Zahra Attamimi's 'The Map of Home' appeared in *Antipodes*, June 2021. The poem was previously titled 'The Home'.

Luke Beesley's 'Albedo' appeared in *The Weekend Australian*, April 2021.

Tony Birch's 'The Eight Truths of Bhouta Khan' appeared in his collection *Whisper Songs*, University of Queensland Press, May 2021.

Peter Boyle's 'Crowded out' appeared in *Australian Book Review*, August 2020.

Lachlan Brown's 'Wish' appeared in Australian Poetry's chapbook *Transforming My Country*, June 2021.

Pam Brown's '(crossing my mind)' appeared in her collection *Endings & Spacings*, Never Never Books, 2021.

Joanne Burns' 'humidicribs' appeared in *Rabbit* 32, April 2021.

Michelle Cahill's 'Variations after Vallejo, and Donald Justice' appeared in *The Weekend Australian*, December 2020.

Derek Chan's '[Immigration Interview: *Chinese Exclusion Act 1882*]' appeared in *Cordite Poetry Review*, October 2020.

Eileen Chong's 'In My Fortieth Year, I Realise I Am Not Like Them' appeared in *Overland*'s Friday Poem series, July 2020.

Louise Crisp's 'Flight paths' appeared in her collection *Glide*, Puncher & Wattmann, February 2021.

Judith Nangala Crispin's 'On finding Charlotte in the Anthropological record' won the Blake Poetry Prize 2020 and appeared in casulapowerhouse.com.

Josie/Jocelyn Deane's 'Waves' appeared in *EnbyLife,* August 2020.

Shastra Deo's 'How to Love Like a Horse' appeared in *Scum Mag*, November 2020.

Dave Drayton's 'x+' was shortlisted for the Blake Poetry Prize 2020, and appeared in casulapowerhouse.com.

Jonathan Dunk's 'Ghost Song (Melbourne, 2020)' appeared in *Red Room Poetry*, October 2020.

Ali Cobby Eckermann and *Joy Harjo*'s 'STORY TREE' appeared in *Red Room Poetry*, March 2021.

Huda Fadlelmawla's 'My Mother's Keeper' won the Australian Poetry Slam QLD Final, 2020.

Michael Farrell's '"Fire" at the Pointer Sisters Factory' appeared in *Blackbox Manifold* 25, Winter 2020.

Liam Ferney's 'The Roaring Twenties' appeared in *Meanjin,* Spring 2020.

Zenobia Frost's 'sandwiches' appeared in *Overland* 240, Spring 2020.

Lou Garcia-Dolnik's 'Don't Call Us Dirty' was shortlisted for the Blake Poetry Prize 2020 and appeared in casulapowerhouse.com.

Juan Garrido-Salgado's 'The dilemma of writing a few verses' appeared in *The Saturday Paper,* May 2021.

Jake Goetz's 'Farming kelp for a reparative state' appeared in *Otoliths* 61, May 2021.

Elena Gomez's 'In Abbotsford, 4pm' appeared in her chapbook *Crushed Silk*, Rosa Press, 2020.

Lisa Gorton's 'MIRABILIA' appeared in *Australian Poetry Journal* 10.1, November 2020.

Charmaine Papertalk Green's 'Familiar Lines' was performed on the podcast *Extraordinary Voices For Extraordinary Times,* episode 3, September 2020.

Natalie Harkin's 'anneal this breath' was commissioned for the exhibition *Yhonnie Scarce: Missile Park* at the Australian Centre for Contemporary Art, and appeared in *The Saturday Paper,* March 2021.

Lujayn Hourani's 'i am writing in vignettes because all we have are fragments' appeared in *Running Dog*, May 2021.

Noémie Huttner-Koros' 'Anthropocene Poetics Part 2' won the Venie Holmgren Poetry Prize 2020 and appeared in *Rabbit* 31, 2020.

Andy Jackson's 'Unrecognised' appeared in *The Saturday Paper*, October 2020.

Jill Jones' 'Possible Manners Of Revelation' appeared in *Otoliths* 58, August 2020 and subsequently in her collection, *Wild Curious Air* (Recent Work Press, 2020).

John Kinsella's 'Exoskeletons' was a runner-up in the Gwen Harwood Poetry Prize 2020 and appeared in *Island* 161, March 2021.

Yeena Kirkbright's 'Mnemonic 2020' appeared in *Overland* 241, Summer 2020.

Louis Klee's 'Actually Existing Australia' appeared in *Australian Book Review*, October 2020. The phrase 'no time is ever resolved' comes from a speech by Jeanine Leane delivered early 2020 in Cambridge.

Shari Kocher's 'Poem whose semiotics of arrival' was runner-up in the Melbourne Poets Union International Poetry Competition 2020.

Abbra Kotlarczyk and *Debris Facility*'s 'Micröbius Tract(ion)' appeared in *un Magazine* 15.1, May 2021.

Kristen Lang's 'Arrival' appeared in her collection *Earth Dwellers*, Giramondo Publishing, March 2021.

Jeanine Leane's 'Native Grasses' appeared in *Australian Poetry Journal* 10.1, November 2020.

Bella Li's 'Juneau' appeared in *Australian Poetry Journal* 10.1, November 2020.

Kate Lilley's 'Wrongs of Woman (after Mary Wollstonecraft) appeared in *Borderless: A transnational anthology of feminist poetry*, Recent Work Press, 2021.

Grace Lucas-Pennington's 'SUPERPOSITION' won the Nakata Brophy Prize 2020 and appeared in *Overland* 239, Winter 2020.

Kent MacCarter's 'Fat Chance #7' appeared in *Westerly* 66.1, June 2021.

Kate Middleton's *'from* Television' appeared in *Island* 161, March 2021.

Peter Minter's 'These Old Bones of Mine' appeared in *Cordite Poetry Review*, May 2021.

Audrey Molloy's 'The Important Things' appeared in *Measures of Truth: 2020 Newcastle Poetry Prize Anthology*, October 2020, and then in her collection *The Important Things*, The Gallery Press, June 2021.

Jazz Money's 'mardi gras rainbow dreaming' appeared in *un Magazine* 15.1, May 2021.

David Musgrave's 'Letter to a Dead Parent' was performed as part of the seminar series 'Notes From a Biscuit Tin', University of Wollongong, April 2021.

Jennifer Nguyen's 'October 3rd 2020' appeared in *Poet Laureates of Melbourne*, October 2020.

Damen O'Brien's 'Aum Shinriko Farms Sarin' won the Melbourne Poets Union International Poetry Competition 2020.

Thuy On's 'Hyphenated' appeared in *Cordite Poetry Review*, February 2021.

Kaya Ortiz's 'Assimilation is not my name' appeared in *Pulch Mag*, September 2020.

Ouyang Yu's 'Advice to a translator of Australian poetry' appeared in his collection *Terminally Poetic*, Ginninderra Press, July 2020.

Luke Patterson's 'Authority of Creeks' appeared in *Running Dog*, November 2020.

Anupama Pilbrow's 'Watching a Simulation of the Birth of the Universe Poem' appeared in *Liminal*, January 2021.

Isabel Prior's 'The Crayfish' appeared in *Westerly* 65.1, July 2020.

Jinghua Qian's 'Still Life' was commissioned for Assembly for the Future and appeared in *The Saturday Paper*, September 2020. The phrase 'already dead' comes from Sherene Razack via Alison Whittaker writing in *The Guardian*; the phrase 'wheat but not bread, fruit but not wine' comes from Daniel Lavery in *Something That May Shock and Discredit You*, attributed to his friend Julian.

Ursula Robinson-Shaw's 'The Ordinary Poem' appeared in *Overland*'s Friday Poem Series, August 2020.

Gig Ryan's 'Simaetha' appeared in *Australian Book Review*, December 2020.

Omar Sakr's 'A Muslim, Christmas' appeared in *Cordite Poetry Review*, May 2021.

Sara M Saleh's 'Border Control: Meditations' won the *Overland* Judith Wright Poetry Prize for New and Emerging Poets 2020 and appeared in *Overland* 242, Autumn 2021.

Mykaela Saunders' 'Sandstone Academy' appeared in *Rabbit* 32, April 2021.

Jaya Savige's 'Her Late Hand' appeared in *The Weekend Australian*, 17 October 2020, and in his collection *Change Machine*, University of Queensland Press, August 2020.

Brooke Scobie's 'Bidjigal Double Brick Dreaming' was runner-up in the *Overland* Judith Wright Poetry Prize for New and Emerging Poets 2020 and appeared in *Overland* 242, Autumn 2021.

Melinda Smith's 'eyelashes' appeared in her collection *Manhandled*, Recent Work Press, September 2020.

Snack Syndicate's 'love song' appeared in *Overland*'s Friday Poem series, May 2021.

Danny Silva Soberano's 'Conman' appeared in *Australian Poetry Journal* 10.1, November 2020.

David Stavanger's 'Seafaring' appeared in *Rabbit* 32, April 2021.

Emily Stewart's 'New Year's Eve Eve' appeared in *Minarets* 11, August 2020.

Andrew Sutherland's 'Arrival Time (in fifteen movements)' appeared in *Westerly* 65.2, November 2020.

Dominic Symes' 'Buried Verse' appeared in *Social Alternatives* 39.3, August 2020.

Heather Taylor-Johnson's 'No Matter How Much Skin I Lose I Am Always the Same Body' appeared in *Not Very Quiet*, March 2021.

Sarah Temporal's '91 Days' appeared in *Cordite Poetry Review*, October 2020.

Shirley Kngwarraye Turner's 'Family are like rocks' appeared in *Arelhekenhe Angkentye: Women's Talk: Poems of Lyapirtneme from Arrernte Women in Central Australia*, Running Water Community Press, August 2020.

Lucy Van's 'Australian Open 1' appeared in her collection *The Open*, Cordite Books, January 2021.

Dženana Vucic's 'my fathers tell me of water' appeared in *Meanjin*, Autumn 2021.

Tais Rose Wae's 'Oysters' appeared in *Westerly* 66.1, June 2021.

Aileen Marwung Walsh's 'White Blankets' appeared in *Westerly* 65.1, July 2020.

Ania Walwicz's 'WHAT HAPPENED TO BOOKS?' appeared in *Rabbit* 32, April 2021.

Alison Whittaker's 'guided meditation ASMR — your therapist's intern calms you down roleplay — monotonous colonial apocalypse comfort ASMR #RoadTo100K' appeared in *Cordite Poetry Review*, May 2021.

Jessica L Wilkinson's 'Heating and Cooling in the Time of Isolation' was highly commended in the Gwen Harwood Poetry Prize 2020 and appeared in *Island* 161, March 2021.

Grace Yee's 'for the chinese merchants of melbourne' appeared in *Westerly* 65.2, November 2020, and won the journal's annual Patricia Hackett Prize.

Printed in Australia
AUHW021009091221
356772AU00001B/1